Lovers Dancing

A Play

Charles Dyer

Samuel French – London
New York – Sydney – Toronto – Hollywood

LOVERS DANCING

Presented at the Albery Theatre, London, on 18th October, 1983, by Doris Cole Abrahams and Leon Becker for Albion Productions Ltd, by arrangement with Ian B. Albery, with the following cast:

Alicia	Jane Carr
Albert	Paul Eddington
George	Colin Blakely
Cheryl	Georgina Hale

Directed by Donald McWhinnie
Setting by Peter Rice

The action takes place in the sitting-room at George and Cheryl's rich-looking home

ACT I   SCENE 1   An Autumn night
       SCENE 2   After dinner

ACT II   Ten minutes later

Time—the present

ACT I

SCENE 1

The satisfied sitting-room at George and Cheryl's rich-looking home. An Autumn night

There is a fireplace L with an electric fire in the hearth and a silver trophy prominent on the mantelpiece. In front of the fireplace is a goatskin rug with a pouffe and jardinière, containing a potted plant, downstage of this. On display shelves UL are various nude male figurines and in front of these stands a small French chair. C is a "pumpfy" sofa with cushions and a glass table with its onyx ashtray. Across an un-used door DR, facing upstage, is a small easel with a large shrouded painting. Downstage of the doorway is a small cabinet containing a hi-fi unit and in front of this an armchair. UR is a console table on which is a framed baby photograph and a tray with four glasses and a bottle of champagne. Next to the table is a pedestal with a nude male statuette. Pillars are each side of an archway (which is offset to the R, running diagonally across the stage). Beyond, and up a step, is the hallway with its sweeping staircase. Against the back wall is a second French chair and a display cabinet

When the CURTAIN rises Albert is standing upon George's cherished goatskin rug; he wears a mackintosh and galoshes. Alicia has been waiting in the hallway, and now she takes off her outdoor coat and drapes it over the French chair

Alicia (*timidly calling*) Chery-y-yl?
Albert (*shouting*) Geo-o-rge!

Alicia moves into the room. Albert catches sight of something moving on the floor. He follows it with his eyes across to the corner DL

Aha! That spider has passed us three times since we arrived. (*Pointing*) Big spider.
Alicia Oogh, I'm not too struck by spiders. (*Skirt-clutched, she hurries to Albert*)
Albert I've grown relatively fond of him. I feel he's one of us. (*Shouting*) Geo-o-orge!
Alicia (*calling*) Chery-y-yl!
Albert (*turning to glare at the silver trophy*) I sense this trophy singeing my neck; frying the lump in my throat. Daresay I am hyper-sensitive over tonight's anniversary: our nineteenth after the Dreadful Bed.
Alicia Oogh, I wish *you* had won a cup. I need nothing more than your fulfilment, Albert-pet. (*She hugs his arm. As always, she speaks with great warmth, with a fierce and stifling love*) If you had won a trophy, I'd burst

out laughing in weird moments. I'd laugh at life's little necessities; you know, at funny cheeses in that delicatessen. And I'd laugh at flowers. Oogh, I'd have hysterics in Woolworths.

Albert You are such an odd little wife, Alicia.

Alicia But haven't you suffered, though?

Albert (*nodding*) I've had three a.m. thoughts all day. We only had a gumboil and two corns. And now I have treading-on-nuts twinges in my feet-balls. (*He crosses to* RC, *stamping his feet*)

Alicia You must have done something at medical school for feet-balls.

Albert No. (*Indrawn breath*) No-ogh. I recall, ah, osteitis and acute osteo-myelitis. And a danger of osteomalacia—or was that for under-privileged women? (*Vehemently*) I am so second-rate, second-rate.

Alicia Shhh. (*Hurrying to him*) You are not. You are first-rate, Albert. And you are beautiful.

Albert No, you are beautiful, Alicia. (*He pats her hand*) I—am merely pretty.

Alicia I had treading-on-nuts pains in our dancing days: sort of a twisted bluey-greenish feeling.

Albert Ah, but my whole being feels yellowy-purple, Alicia. I've tingled all day; couldn't concentrate on Mrs Anstruther's gumboil.

Alicia Should you take another pill or something?

Albert I am not ailing, Alicia. No, I'm closer to hungering. (*He shivers: scrubs at his stomach*)

Alicia Tummy ache?

Albert No, no, Alicia. Apprehensive-ache. Yes, (*moving upstage behind the sofa*) I am apprehensive. (*Yelling*) Geo-o-o-orge!

Alicia Chery-y-yl!

Albert Years in, years out—no matter how late *we* are, George and Cheryl are always later. (*He rests against the sofa arm to massage his ankle*) My feet-balls could be psychological. Yes! Pseudocyesis, Alicia. Ghost preg-nancy. Very apt for George. (*Dramatically, he points at the trophy*) George cut those buttons. I *know* he cut the threads of those buttons. *The* buttons. Oh, the pain of mind!

Albert covers his face. Alicia hurries to him

Alicia Mustn't be bitter, Albert-pet; not after nineteen years.

Albert Psychological. Yes. These twingey feet-balls are a psychological manifestation, because of the inevitable vigil when visiting George and Cheryl. (*Bellowing*) Cheryl!

Alicia (*shouting*) George!

Albert Yes. Mere mention of Cheryl fetches a change in the pigmentation of my nipples. (*He hugs his chest*) I shall give birth in that damn'n blasted silver cup.

Alicia (*moving upstage*) They can be quite warm folk in themselves.

Albert George is warm. Cheryl is on heat.

Alicia (*giggling*) Oogh, isn't she just. (*She nods at the easel*) And I wonder how many more naked soldiers?

Albert Naked armies you mean. Oh damn, I'm so tiny-minded. Tiny-minded, I am.

Alicia You're not. (*She returns to him; hugs his arm*) Big, you are. Big-minded.

Albert Glycholic and taurocholic. There are the salts of my jealousy. They are the burning in my heart, Alicia. Hello! There he goes again!

Together, they follow the spider's progress, as it scrabbles in a circle and back to its corner DL

Home safe. It could be so wonderful, Alicia: to be safe home. You and me. Crackling fire. Dog. Slippers. Our own spider. And our own little boy.

Alicia puts her fingers to Albert's lips. He nods. Gently, he takes away her fingers; then pats them between his hands

George (*off, upstairs*) I bet he *is*.

Alicia Sssh. Here's George coming down.

George (*off, upstairs*) And furthermore—Albert never wipes his feet.

George enters down the stairs. He crosses the hall and out of sight UR. *Immediately, he returns and guiltily peeps round the pillar at them*

Oh, you've arrived. How nice, ha ha. (*Moving into the room*) Are you potty?—why didn't you give us a shout?

Albert Who doesn't wipe his feet, George?

George Oh 'ell—well, you never do, Albert. (*To Alicia*) Does he, darlin'? Aw, see her little shinin' face. Give us a kiss, you cheeky hussy.

George kisses Alicia's cheek. Then he ushers her towards the hallway, bundles her coat (from the French chair) into her arms, pats her bottom, and steers her up the stairs

Now off upstairs, there's a darlin'. Cheryl is panting for girl-talk.

Alicia Oogh, and I bet she's just drowning in new clothes. (*On the stairs*) I'd die for Cheryl's clothes, I would. I'd smash and grab for Cheryl's clothes.

Alicia exits excitedly up the stairs

Albert The Gospel according to George and Cheryl?

George Sardonic, are we? Sardonic?

Albert Why should my wife race to the feet of yours?

George To primp and fluff in our boudoir. Can't bring our boudoir down here, can they?

Albert And forever plausible. Amen. (*He removes his mackintosh and drapes it over the sofa-back*)

George Would you have a care! Our brocade might damage your mackintosh. (*Glaring, and with distasteful fingers, he picks up Albert's mackintosh*) Aw!—and look at your goloshers, Albert-darlin'. You haven't desecrated my home with goloshers, have you? Get up your hooves.

Albert rests a hand against the left sofa-arm. Gruntingly, George tugs off Albert's galoshes

S'like shoeing a mule. All this is your wall-to-wall pure Wilton, for God's sake. (*Rising, he shakes the galoshes under Albert's nose*) Anyhow — goloshers'll make your feet ache.
Albert (*brightly*) I hadn't thought of that!

George removes the mackintosh and galoshes out of sight in the hall UR

(*Wandering on to the goatskin rug*) Did you know you had a spider in your dust, George? Wonder if he's weeping for our nineteenth anniversary?

George returns

George And will Alicia be weeping all through our Night of the Dreadful Bed?
Albert She'll always weep, George.
George Would you have a care on that fur rug? It's white mountain goatskin.
Albert But I've always stood here. Every time we call, I stand on this particular spot.
George Yes; and for your edification, Albert, there's a dirty mark there.
Albert Fancy that! (*He steps aside*) Have you bought a goatskin rug to cover my dirty marks?

George stoops, clucking, and fussily straightens his rug

George Anyhow!

George joins Albert. They stand side by side, uncomfortably, facing the audience

(*Gustily*) So how are you, you old bugger, eh, eh?
Albert Quite excellent, George. Are you well?
George Not double-bad, darlin'; not double-bad.

George indulges in a tuneless whistle (a habit of his), or it might be a pompahdy-pom singing sound. Albert ponders the room in envy

Pom-pahdy-pahdy-pom-pom-pom. (*Jovially*) So you're all right, then, eh, eh!
Albert Splendid, yes, yes. And you are all right?
George Like a bomb, darlin', yes, yes. Medical racket booming, is it? Medical racket?
Albert Fair, George, yes. Fair. How is your factory?
George Middling good, Albert; yes, middling. We're expanding, you know. Expanding.
Albert Very nice.
George Pom-pahdy-pahdy-pom-pom. . . . So! You're all right, you cheeky bugger, eh, eh? Ho ho. All right, are you?
Albert Reasonable, George, considering. And you are expanding.
George Business is double-smashin'. I mean, it is gigantic, darlin'.
Albert Nice.
George And you're on top, you old sod. Eh, eh, eh? Ha ha.
Albert To be honest, George . . .

George (*gloomily*) Oh.
Albert I've had dread atmospheres of unfulfilment.
George Oh 'ell. (*He puts his hand to his brow*)
Albert Headache, George?
George No, Albert, no. But we haven't reached the toast, yet. The toast. But you've started your grumbles.
Albert You did ask me. You asked me.
George (*nodding*) Every minute one's born.

Albert, with doctor-patient atmospheres, brings a pen-torch from his pocket

Albert (*in bedside tones*) Shall we see those eyes, old lad?
George Shall we 'ell! Get off! (*Shading his eyes, he moves away*) Continue with your unfulfilments.
Albert I am not grousing, George.
George You're not, uhugh, uhugh. Pom-pahdy-pahdy-pom-pom-pom-pom.
Albert You are not looking at me, George.

George sighs; elaborately swings to face Albert—who turns away

I am in a somewhat ah, premature menopause as-it-were, George. My mind has a middle-aged thread, temple to temple, which tightens with each anniversary of our Dreadful Bed Night. (*He circles the sofa*) I would rise above the years—I know I could, were I able to drag some glory from my mind. I *do* sense a little greatness up here; but how do I clutch it? What are its genes? How do I analyse it; tear it from my mind, and shape it? How do I open my doors, George? How? How, George? (*Hammering the sofa back with each "how"*) How! How! How!

George is appalled. He hurries across to smooth the sofa-back material

George Have a care, have a care!
Albert I need a message for my life, George. A speck of glory. Fulfilment, George—just a whiff. To—oh, to discover a mortal secret: just a tiny secret, and name it; to be consulted by leaders—on a humblest point; but have an answer at the nth moment. To invent something; or to . . . (*he rests un-seeing eyes upon the shrouded easel*) . . . or to paint something.
George That's one of Cheryl's. Did it herself. Cheryl.

But Albert is glazed by his own problem

Albert To be heard, George. To be heard; to create; to compose music, just a little song—then catch it on a distant crackle from Samarkand. Ahhh. . . . But I know I'm not clever enough; and I *want* to be, before it's too late. I *want* to be. (*Banging the sofa-back again*) I want, I *want*, I want.
George (*fussily smoothing the cloth*) Blaming our sofa, are you; blaming our sofa?
Albert Sorry, George. But it's splitting my mind, this frustrated black thread. (*He flops into the sofa*)
George But, my old enchantin' darlin'—*you* are a respected man. You are the village chemist. *Our chemist.* (*He sits beside Albert*)

Albert Mm. I daresay I could find vague peace—if they were not building a hypermarket down the street, and thrusting a motorway up my back passage. (*Absently, he is fiddling with the onyx ashtray from the glass table. He slaps it and rubs it*)

George You are fiddlin' with our onyx.

Albert Sorry? Oh! (*He laughs*) I thought you meant some animal with horns.

George grabs the ashtray; he polishes it with his handkerchief

George This cost a bomb; takes special cream for cleaning it. And you've been steeped in pills and chemicals all day. (*He replaces the ashtray on the glass table*)

Albert So here I am. Sorry, ah—sorry, George; but it helps to worry aloud with someone. And Alicia tends to smother me in a fluff of love and incomprehension.

George Uhugh. Pom-pahdy-pahdy-pom-pom . . .

Albert (*doctor-wise*) Have you been sleeping well, old lad?

George No. I've been screaming through the nights on black thread. We're all middle-aged, y'know.

Albert Your lips are a mite blue.

George Get off staring at my lips! (*He covers his mouth*) Do it on purpose, do you? On purpose?

Albert No no no no.

George (*swinging to face him*) Because you lost the toss? Lost the toss? Destroying my health for revenge?

Albert Force of habit, George. I *am* a chemist; and I was almost ah—almost ah . . .

George We all know you're an Almost-Ah, Albert. Can't you forget your unfulfilment, just for the nineteenth? If you want glory, you have to aim for glory.

Albert I am aiming. I *said* I was aiming. But I can't find the target.

George Oh 'ell! (*He slumps deeper into the sofa*)

Albert My heart is screaming for keys. *Keys.* (*He rises, crosses to* L *and stands on the rug*) But I can't even find the doors of my mind—because my mind has died, George. It's dead. My mind is dead.

George You are standing upon our goatskin rug. The mountain goatskin *rrrr*ug, Albert.

Albert Sorry. (*He steps off the rug*) You see, I *know* that *somewhere*—maybe but one in a worldful—but somewhere is a *genius* who could be trapped in a giant vinegar bottle. Trapped in a vinegar bottle, wearing nothing but spiked boots; and he would scramble to safety. . . . I believe this, George. Not a decent man, perhaps: perhaps a heartless man, uncaring, with stone eyes and loose lips; *but he'd win!* He would gutsy-well win. He would ah— oh, heaven-knows—he'd clamp his slobbery mouth to the glass, and *suck.* Yes! And by sheer (*he fist punches the air with each "suck"*) *suck* after *suck* after *suck* . . . (*he ends on a huge intake of breath*) . . . he'd *sssssuck* his way to freedom. (*He nods awhile; sighs*) But you would not understand, George. (*He moves to the sofa-arm nearest George*)

George Would I not; oh no no. How could Blue-Lipped George appreciate humanity.

Albert Well how could you? How can you assimilate my shriekings for glory, when you sit amongst furs and rich trappings?

George Uhugh. Uhugh. (*He nods*) Well, Albert, I reckon your spot o' glory ... (*he sucks his tooth, then squints*) ... would be like that Quazzimoddy, that Quazzimoddy-fella.

Albert Charles Laughton, yes. Hunchback of Notre-Dame.

George That's the lad. And that gypsy girl on the scaffold; and the poor, hump-ed, slobbery bugger—just as they're about to slit her gullet—wheeeeeeeee! And down he swings on a woppin' rope from the Cathedral turrets; and "Sanctuary!" he screams.

Albert Yes. YES.

George Sanctuary!

Albert joins in excitedly

Albert ⎫
George ⎭ (*shouting together*) Sanctuary! Sanctuary!

Albert This is it!

George And the bells chime; the choirs sing!

Albert And he *sucks* her to glory. By heavens, George, yes yes yes!

George (*rising*) A dream, Albert. It's a paper dream; doesn't exist, darlin'.

Albert It existed for you. *You won the toss.*

George I see, I see. Pom-pahdy-pahdy-pom-pom. (*He glowers at Albert; steps over his rug to* L)

Albert I am not harking back.

George You're not. Uhugh.

Albert But you *are* lucky, George; you and Cheryl You have tasted glory.

George Lucky! I *am* that bugger from your vinegar bottle. (*Carefully, he steps back over his rug*) Literally. Had you forgotten my dad was a glass-blower; and me, ten years in the melting shop? I spit glass when I cough. And Cheryl-the-darlin', her father collected whisky bottles for his hobby: a pub pianist, he was, with TB and hammer fingers. Cheryl had no knickers when I first saw her.

Albert She had no knickers——(*He stops himself*) Oh give over, George. You two—if you stuck a tent peg in mud you'd strike oil.

George God almighty! (*Affronted, he appeals to the gods*) They shade their eyes from my bleeding fingers, and call it luck.

Albert I am not belittling you, George. Always I said you'd make good. Oh yes. "George'll get there," I said. Oh, no problem. (*Comfortably*) No, no, I had complete faith.

George Optimists—are the curse o' the world. "George'll be all right." But George has *his* black threads; George dreams, and screams in his mind. George breaks his back, fingers, teeth and gums, scramblin' for a crumb; then IF-bloody-if George makes it: "Oh, I knew he'd do it," says Albert. And all achievement is quashed. Typical.

Albert (*mooching downstage of the sofa*) Forever a tempestuous so-and-so, you were.

George (*to the gods*) And he turns his back when I explain. (*Imitating Albert*) You're not loooking at me, Albert.

Albert (*swinging round*) Grammar school lad—that was you. Your dad had shares in that bottle factory of yours. There has been a lot given you, George; oh yes, a lot has been done for you. (*He points to the Louis-Philippe style jardinière* DL) I remember that aspidistra-thing at your mother's place.

George Aspidistra! It's Louis Sank, you sod! (*He steps to* L *over his rug, in a movement of frustration; then he returns to* LC, *stepping over it again*) Well, at least I snatched my opportunities, and tore at 'em, chewed 'em, and spat 'em in the teeth o' Fate, by hell. . . . And I remember *your* mother's place. (*Sing-song*) "Albert's gone to medical school. Albert's gone to medical school. Dah dee dah dee dah dah." (*He blows a raspberry*)

Albert Yes, rub it in, rub it in.

George (*forcefully*) You had the balls of greatness in your hands; and crushed 'em. Destroyed yourself. So now you're a grizzling, grumblin', niggling, whining . . . aw hell!

Albert S'all right, s'all right. Finish it: failed doctor. Failed doctor and second-rate chemist. (*Seemingly, he has a masochistic urge to hear his failures voiced aloud. He utters a sad, hoarse cry, and flops into the sofa*)

George This year, I swore to myself I wouldn't tell you. But you made me, didn't you? You managed it. Switched *my* glories to *your* martyrdom. Hell, it's clever. (*He sniffs, and paces awhile; then offers a sudden hand-of-détente*)

Albert We shall not fret, George. (*Shaking hands*) We shall not fret.

George I shouldn't have said it, though. (*Flopping down beside Albert*) Shouldn't have said it, darlin'. But I'm sometimes choked with vengeance. Vengeance, Albert. My gorge bubbles over at the world's—well—supplicants. So I—you know—seek a kind of vengeance. (*He sniffs, frowns and nods*) Not a bang at our door, nor letter, nor telephone-tinkle which isn't somebody *wanting* somethin'. If it's not Our Dumb Animals or an exploding bill—it's "Hello George!" And (*he gives a frustrated growl*); and I shrink from the Feed-me, Guide-me, Help-me, Save-me-Show-me. (*He gives a big sigh*) Same at my bottle factory: no greeting, no gesture without hopes of reward. "Want a smoke, George?" "Drink, George?" "Cushion, George?" "Shall I pray for you, George?" . . . "Jump on my face, George! I like it, George. Jump on my face and give us the money." It's a clutching parade of grovelling supplicants, until I shout Christ Christ Christ! Vomit vomit vomit . . .! And they call me a peculiar man. (*He shakes his head, and sniffs glumly*) I'd kiss the feet—and God send the day—of a fella who spat in my eye and farted in my face for nothin'.

Long pause

Albert Difficult, but I could try.

George Wasn't meaning you, Albert.

Albert Much obliged. Alicia and I hadn't quite seen ourselves as grovelling supplicants.

George You're a proud man, me darlin'. I know that. Hellfire, you wouldn't crawl to me for anything. You wouldn't—(*less confidently*)—would you?

Albert Don't be insulting.

George Oh, I blurt my thoughts; then hate myself. I was awake at three this morning, remembering how evil I am. Evil. D'you recall Ma Calthropp, at all?

Albert Good heavens! Didn't the headmaster punish our whole class?

George (*nodding*) Some rotten little whelp tipped manure into Ma Calthropp's scullery.

Albert So it was you!

George (*nodding*) Me. I did it. Poor Ma Calthropp: shrivelled mummy; skin o' rotten peaches, she had; kidneys to hell; gum-champing and cold, she was; and ankle deep in manure. (*He is brow-creased in regret; then he bursts into uncontrollable laughter, which changes back to sadness*) God, I detest myself. (*Savagely, he rises; and paces*) Slugs trail my mind. Slime trails. (*From the table* UR, *he picks up the framed photograph*) To think I was once a baby. And now, I live with evil flashes. Behind my eyes. I summon them myself. I know I hate remembering; but in they zoom. (*He comes downstage and turning the picture sideways, considers his reflection in the glass*) And I look evil. I do. Don't I! (*Plaintively, he turns to Albert*) How evil do I look?

Albert Ah ... (*He rises and goes and peers over George's shoulder at the reflections in the picture*)

George Just an opinion. Not a quantity survey.... *Why am I confessing to you, anyway?*

Albert No, no, let me help, George, please. I did well on my Psychology (*He takes the picture from George; sets it on the glass table* C. *Then, doctorwise*) Now. What species of evil are we seeking, old lad?

George (*sardonically*) Flesh-rotting, under-the-arm and debauched. (*Sadly*) Oh, Albert ... all the errors and embarrassments of my life; the tactlessnesses, binges, cock-ups; the stains of body and mind which I've imprinted upon the minds and bodies of others. God Almighty! (*He swings away upstage, then comes back again*) All right. Do I look clean, then? *Clean*, Albert. I mean, I mean.... (*Moving closer; confidentially*) Do I—do I smell? Do I smell, Albert? There's no-one else I could ask.

Albert sniffs tentatively

Albert (*brightly*) Quite pleasant. What is it?

George Splash-on freshner. I'd get by, would I?

Albert (*nodding*) Smell-wise. Surely.

George But age-wise, darlin'? Am I young enough? *Enough*, I mean, *enough*?

Albert I should say that ah, for your age, weight and habits, you were, ah, reasonable. Yes.

George Reasonable's hardly encouraging.

Albert You look tired.

George You don't give much, do you! (*He swings upstage*)

Albert (*following*) *You don't need much.*

George Everyone needs something, Albert—somethin' he hasn't bought.

Albert You *do* have something you haven't bought.
George Don't, Albert!
Albert Something you *stole*.
George Don't add a thing. D'you follow?
Albert ⎱ *(together)* ⎰ You stole my life.
George ⎰   ⎱ NO! No, I said.
George It'll be hard enough at the toast. Recriminations and tears.
Albert (*bitterly*) Eighteen years old.
George NO, I said! Just pretend. Smile and pretend. Hey! (*Moving to Albert, he sets a jovial arm round Albert's shoulder*) Think of your supper, darlin'. There's your drop o' bubbly, and your lobster delight. Ho ho, you what!
Albert M'yes.
George Your enthusiasm is dazzlin'. (*Snatching his baby-picture from the glass table, he returns it to the table* UR) Cheryl's slaved over a feast for you buggers tonight. Exotic meat with your champers, to say nothin' of your Lymeswold. And what'll *you* say when you've scoffed it? Sweet fanny. We'll be lucky to fetch a belch, leave alone a compliment.
Albert (*moving behind the sofa*) Is this an example of your evil behaviour?
George We-ell, it shrivels my spleen, your purposeful disinterest in *my* glories. Tramplin' your goloshers over our Wilton; scuffing our brocade with your mackintosh. Just a tiddly "Oh, that's a nice rug" or "Oh, new wallpaper, George?" or "What lovely puddin', Cheryl". Would it cripple you? Eh? Eh? But no. You haven't even glanced at Cheryl's painting here; and . . . (*he clears his throat, then moves* DR, *strangely self-conscious*) . . . and, it's beautiful.
Albert M'yes, we've been hearing of Cheryl's paintings. The whole village is buzzing over Cheryl's paintings.

Pause. Albert moves slowly towards the easel

Is that a naked man? That painting?

George laughs with assumed derision

Is it? Is it a naked soldier, George?
George It's a—a life study, yes.
Albert Naked man.
George Hellfire. (*Crossing to* C) We have naked *beaches* the other side of, um, other side o' what's-it. Everyone bouncin' and danglin'.
Albert For swimming, yes. Swimming.
George (*scornfully patient*) Cheryl—has a group of housewives. Right? She is one of a group. I mean, I've built them a studio in our paddock. I'd show you, if you had any true interest: Swedish maple, redwood and glass, northern light; lovely. And um, well they um—Cheryl supplies buns'n tea, and they um, natter and do a spot o' daubing.

Albert raises his eyebrows

And yes—(*a little cough*)—they do an occasional life class. A life class, yes. It was good enough for Leo de um, Leo-de-Whatsit, wasn't it? Harmless hobby. Village housewives.

Albert They have soldiers from the camp.
George There may have been *a* soldier.
Albert Young, naked soldiers.
George I know. (*Wretchedly*) *I know.*

Pause. George mooches across to the armchair

I know. Firm and young, with blue-white new eyes. Supple flesh. Taut
flanks and flat bellies. And they call me Sir; or *Dad.* (*He flops into the
armchair*) But they're nice lads. I'm not bothered. Pom-pahdy-pahdy-
pom-pom-pom . . .

Albert moves DR, *arms folded. Then with a professional finger to his lip, he
gazes down at George*

(*Squinting up at Albert*) Yes, I know. And I *have* noticed the odd tyke of
greasy hair'n slouchy eyes, smelling of hot, damp biscuit. And there's one
I wouldn't trust with a stuffed otter. . . . But—nice lads in the main. Nice
lads.
Albert Nineteen anniversaries—with me pretending Michael is mine; pretending I'm his dad. *It must screw your heart out, George.* Why've you let
Cheryl drag us all here? And three months early this year.
George That's to take in his coming-of-age, darlin'. You're the gynaecolo-
whatsit, aren't you?
Albert And you're the husband. Put your foot down. Why don't you?
George Oh to hell! (*Rising angrily; crossing to* C) Because! Because I have to
confirm, Albert-darlin'. I daren't argue. (*Plaintively*) I don't think she
maybe loves me any more. I built her these pillars, and this mansion, and I
don't think she loves me, Albert. Don't think she loves me.

*Alicia hurries down the stairs. Inadequately, she is wearing one of Cheryl's
old outfits, dress and matching handbag. She moves* DL, *happily primping*

Alicia Cheryl wants you boys to fetch in the old familiar trunk.
George Does she, the darlin'? (*He moves into the hallway*)
Albert Were you wearing that dress when we came?
Alicia Isn't it gorgeous? (*She mouths at Albert from behind the handbag*)
Albert Why are you mouthing at me? Is it Cheryl's?
Alicia Gorgeous, Albert, isn't it? Cheryl's given it me; and this gorgeous
handbag.
George Lovely nature, Cheryl has.
Albert Oh, blast to hell. And damn!

Albert strides out UR

George (*astounded*) I'm aghast. Aghast.

George exits UR

Glumly, Alicia moves to the sofa; she sits and sighs

*Off are indistinct rumbles of Albert and George quarrelling. They return,
humping a small trunk between them. They place it* DL; *and they continue*

their quarrel face-to-face across the luggage, speaking with low intensity—
as though Alicia were too young to hear

Albert Unforgiveable.

George Should give your complexes a rest for once.

Albert Cheryl sees herself on a damn royal barge upstairs there. Waggly-waggly fingers; casting her still-warm rags of Sheba at *my wife*.

Alicia (*worriedly*) Ooo-ooogh.

George Don't worry, lovey. (*Then to Albert*) I never knew a man so sick with spiteful envy. That little lovey ran down those stairs in ecstasy, the darlin'. Her little shining face. And those "rags o' Sheba", thank you very much, cost a bloody fortune.

Albert What's wrong with them, then? Last year's, I suppose.

George No. Last week's, you sod.

Albert crosses to Alicia. He sits beside her

Albert Alicia, can't you see you are being patronized?

Alicia I think I look suave, though, and svelte.

George Ravishing, darlin'. Little shining face.

Albert Never mind the crumbs, George. (*Urgently, to Alicia*) We don't need their charity, Alicia.

Alicia (*whispering*) It's dreadfully expensive, Albert; and the handbag's reindeer hide. *Reindeer hide.*

Albert Cheryl'll be down here, all slinky-slinky in shiny new jewels and silks; and you'll be all second-hand in her still-warm cast-offs. *My wife.* At least your own dress is—is your own.

George How's *that* for small-minded.

Alicia I think I look nice, though. I look nice, don't I?

Rising to DR, *Alicia twirls for Albert's benefit; but Albert cannot bring a compliment to his lips*

Say, Albert, say!

George Tell her she's pretty, you chemical sloth.

Albert (*rising*) You're the last one to instruct *me*—on husbandry.

George Get off! Tell her she's divine.

Albert I can't. I can't. I can't.

Albert storms away UR; *George strides to* UL; *and Alicia bursts into tears* DR

Cheryl (*off, from upstairs*) Darlings, darlings, darlings!

Cheryl enters down the stairs—in a whirl of fluff and wiggly fingers and jangly bracelets. All is gush and fuss

I have *so* neglected you all, my sweeties. (*She gazes benignly upon them*) And George! (*She hugs his arm; pecks his cheek*) All those juicy-juicy soldiers have gone. *Gone.* (*She gushes to Albert, takes both his hands and surveys him sexily*) Albert, darling Albert. Oh, look at his cheeky face. And how Alicia grooms you, doesn't she? She keeps you so clean. I do like men to be clean. And you are *clea-ean*, Albert. Mmmm. I adore your withers and flanks, you juicy darling.

She presses her cheek to his lips; Albert pecks her dutifully, gloomily

George (*brightly*) Soldiers gone, have they; gone, have they?

Cheryl Oh my sweeties, they have taken their steam and bluster and occasional *in*conveniences-in-doorways-my-dears, and they have returned us to our god-awful quiet hedges. We are all furious—us girls. But doesn't Alicia look delicious'n *rich*? Here, sweetie!

Moving to Alicia, Cheryl snugly links arms, and cuddles Alicia's hand (looking magnificent in ratio); and she walks Alicia to the fireplace

Isn't she a poem, a sweet poem? Darling, you *must* come to our painting group. George—has built us girls a studio in the paddock. Wouldn't she adore our painting group, George! Oh, we do *exciting* things, Alicia; 'cept the girls are in shreds, darling. Well, no more soldiers, you see. . . .

Cheryl moves between the men, dragging Alicia along

No more early bugles and nightly trumpetings. Flown, my darlings, flown! And Peggy-Thingy is in hysterics. Well—she was *hollow*, Alicia-darling, for our latest Welsh corporal. That's him on the easel. Well, *nearly* him. He isn't finished. (*She wiggles her fingers at the easel*)

Albert Somewhat shrouded, isn't he?

Cheryl You shall see him after dinner, Albert; and you, sweetie. (*Impulsively, she kisses Alicia's cheek; then she plucks fluff from Alicia's frock. Crossing to the fireplace; loudly*) George—you have a stain on your trousers.

George Ah. (*He turns his back; scrubs at the stain*)

Cheryl So, Peggy-Thingy says the camp is empty: simply a mass of crisp-bags, nostalgic tracks in mud, and latrines with flapping doors. Urrrgh.

Albert It'll be a bit awkward, won't it? No soldiers to paint.

Cheryl Not really, Albert. We could paint *you*, my sweet.

Alicia Oogh, and wouldn't he just be wonderful. (*Eagerly*) I'd love a genuine oil of Albert?

George I can't wait.

Alicia Oogh, Cheryl, please! I see him all mysterious in flowing robes against a Jerusalem sky.

Albert Rubbish. (*Hurrying to Alicia*) I'm not Jewish, Alicia.

George Don't apologize, Albert.

Albert I didn't. Only people have sometimes thought I was. Jewish. But I am not Jewish. That is all I said.

Alicia You could pretend, Albert. Oogh, would you, Cheryl? Shielding his eyes from the molten sun. Please, Cheryl.

Albert Don't beg, Alicia!

Cheryl And it isn't quite us, Alicia-sweetie: we're half through Bacchus, at present. You know, with his furry thighs and sweaty flesh. And his horn.

George Zzzzz. Hornzzz, Cheryl-darlin'. Two horns, he had.

Cheryl I was meaning his cornucopia, George-darling. His horn of plenty.

Cheryl crosses to Alicia, takes her hand, and they sit together on the sofa

Oh, but you should have seen our juicy corporal, Alicia, with his natural Welsh bronze flesh. (*She sighs*) All gone. Peggy-Thingy says the commanding officer should have warned us girls. I mean, George has given a fortune to their mess fund.

Albert Paid them as well, did you, George?

George glowers

Cheryl Open the trunk, Albert-sweetie! And do your champagne, George: because we are *there*, darlings. It is long ago and far away. (*Rising, she twirls across to the trunk*)

Albert is crouched there, having thrown open the trunk lid; Cheryl kneels L *of him; and George comes* L *of her*

Alicia (*bottom lip quivering*) Ogh-oggghhh.

George Aw, Cheryl, do we have to drag memories from that old coffin?

Cheryl This was a date, George. A date we all agreed.

George Champers is enough; and a nice supper. Why hang sad numbers on our backs?

Cheryl Here's your sad number, George.

Cheryl produces a tail-suit and slams it into George's arms. Pinned to the back of the jacket is the number 18. *George places the suit over the sofa-back*

And yours, Albert-my-sweetie.

Another tail-suit; this time with the number 19 *pinned to its back. She passes the suit to Albert. He places his suit over the sofa-back as George has done. George goes to open the champagne at the table* UR

Ours are in the bottom, Alicia. Tissue paper. All cleaned and re-textured. Everything as fresh as on that long-long-ago day.

Alicia (*weeping bitterly*) Ogh-ogggghhhh.

Albert There-there, Alicia. There-there.

Cheryl is taking patent leather shoes from the trunk. A pair for George; another for Albert. And now she finds a framed photograph; she hugs it

Cheryl Here is George, winning our trophy. Oh, but look at Alicia's little face, peeping past George's elbow.

Albert That *is* "darling"—actually having *Alicia* on the photograph.

George Don't be bitter, you bugger. (*He pops the cork, and pours*)

Cheryl Wheeee! (*Rising, she sets her photograph on the mantelpiece*) The four of us together; before our final dance; when we were fresh, and *clean* and *new*.

Alicia Oogh. (*She rises and moves upstage blowing her nose*)

George (*handing champagne to Alicia and Albert*) Lucky we had a photo taken; or we mightn't have known there'd ever *been* a dance. *Might we, Albert!*

George has his own glass and now Cheryl takes hers

Cheryl The toast, George. The toast, sweetie.

George Um, yes. Um—well, raise your glasses then to our Michael. Um—
our son Michael. He's um, a good lad. Eighteen tomorrow. And um,
there'll be a natty sports car outside his dormitory.

Cheryl S'all arranged with his housemaster, sweeties.

George A little somethin' on the back seat for you two. I mean, um—*from*
you two. To Michael. You can forget the cash.

Albert Tolerable—since we don't know what we've bought.

Alicia What *have* we bought Michael?

George Um—what did you stick in the back, darlin'?

Cheryl A delicious toiletry set.

*Moving to her, she takes Alicia's hand, and cosily brings Alicia to stand beside
her at the fireplace*

N'awfully manly one in leather.

George Oh yes. Silver-plated talcum thing and stuff.

Cheryl And engraved. "From Uncle Albert and Auntie Alice."

Alicia (*withdrawing her hand*) I like to be called *Alicia*.

George So raise your glasses!

Alicia Albert, I like to be called Alicia. *Alicia*.

Cheryl University, George. University.

George Oh yes. Um . . .

Albert University? University-what?

George Let us trust Michael prospers at um—oh 'ell—at um, university.

Albert Has he a place, then? Is it fixed? What is he reading?

George Oh bloody-ell-and-brimstone!

Cheryl *George!*

*George knocks back his champagne, then strides up and down, pouring himself
another and another*

Albert What is he reading?

Cheryl (*going to him*) Medicine. He's going to be a doctor.

Albert *Is* he!

George I thought *I* was evil; but grinding us into the past like this. Hellfire,
Cheryl.

Alicia Haven't we all suffered enough? Nineteen years. And poor Albert,
too.

George Poor every-bugger.

Albert Why do we tolerate this anniversary ritual? Why are we doing it?

Cheryl We are doing it, my darling—all my sweet sweet darlings, for the girl
who suffered. And we all know who *that* was. *Me!* So raise your glasses,
darlings, and drink to my Michael.

They raise their glasses

I don't know if he's *your* son, George; or if he's *yours*, Albert. But I
bloody know he's mine. To Michael!

Albert }
George } (*together*) To Michael.
Alicia }

And they drink

CURTAIN

SCENE 2

The same. After dinner

The trunk has gone; the men's tail-suits are hanging over the sofa-back. George's pair of patent leather shoes is at one end of the sofa; and Albert's pair are at the L end. There are two goblets of brandy on the glass table

When the CURTAIN *rises George and Albert are standing behind the sofa, buttoning up their dress shirts*

Albert I have no idea why she thinks I am clean. I couldn't say, George. Truly. I feel I am averagely dusty, really.

George I think you're dusty, too. Think you're very dusty.

Albert M'yes. Still, what is clean? To a medical man, maggots are clean.

George Whilst we're on the medical stint, Albert, um, well, one accepts life's dwindlings, sort-of: a stringy vein, or the odd clocking hip; but um, mmm. (*He changes his mind*) Oh, something else I wanted to ask. You've heard the saying "fluff in your navel"?

Albert (*professionally*) Fluff in the umbilicus, m'yes? Perfectly normal, m'yes?

George Normal, is it? Oh thank God. I thought I'd got ectoplasm.

Albert No-o-ogh.

George Only noticed recently. Every morning. Little caches of fluff in the old tummy button. Blue fluff. Green fluff. Yes, ectoplasm I thought I'd got.

Albert and George come round the respective ends of the sofa; they sit in shirt tails to sip their brandy

Um, you've heard the saying "wriggling navels"?

Albert No?

George (*disappointed*) Oh. Well, Cheryl and me—we're not wriggling navels too much, Albert. Do you read me? (*Brightly*) I imagine it's normal at our age, eh?

Albert No, it is not.

George It isn't?

Albert Oh no no no no no.

George (*glumly*) Oh.

Each drinks his brandy; and takes up his white tie. Albert rises, moves forward, and—looking into the "audience mirror"—he fastens on his tie

I'm still viable, Albert. I am viable. By God, you what! Ho ho. Oh yes. (*Now he rises to tie his white tie, standing just behind Albert at the "audience mirror"*) And by hell, there's an itsy-bitsy little hussy with a really cheeky bottom at, um ... what is that shop?

Albert (*tersely*) Radlett's.

George Had you noticed as well, you dirty lecher?

Albert She stocks the shelves.

George Does she? Well how about that for a cheeky bottom, Albert, eh? Eh? Eh? I'll swear she shades in her creases: there's a swingeing line from her tail, down between her cheeks and up until——

Albert (*a deep sigh of frustration*) Oh-h-h-h-ogh. (*He moves back to the sofa; slumps into its L corner, and polishes the patent leather shoes on his shirt-tail*)

George Something getting to you, old darlin'?

Albert If only she had been brilliant and beautiful, George.

George I know who you mean. Alicia.

Albert With golden breasts and honey-blest.

George Pom-phady-pahdy-pom-pom-pom. (*He moves behind the sofa*)

Albert I love her. I mean, I do love Alicia, George.

George Her sweet little face, yes.

Albert But all day I've felt it was a turning time, you see, George. I am consumed from within. Fires are changing my—my gut to melted wax. My blood is bubbling.

George This is no talk for a chemist. (*He comes round to sit beside Albert*)

Albert Just to mention that hussy at Radlett's; you, with your swingeing creases, and down and up . . . and between . . . and her cheeks and tail . . . oh-h-h-h-ogh.

George Most encouraging, Albert. Signs of life. . . . How viable are *you*, then?

Albert Oh my heavens, George! I have a need for diving into Scandinavian pools. Crystal snow. Gods, and blonde-tress-ed women. Big women. (*He rises and moves forward*) Busty-bouncing and long-tress-ed. Diving from the cliffs of Scrag-Elky-Valhalk, with the longboats and the horn-ed trumpets sounding. (*Singing*) Poo-whoo-hoo. Poo-whoo-hoooo. (*Eyes alight, he sees himself as a Viking*) Swoosh into icing waters—to rise again, puffing spray from your scrag-handsome bearded Viking face; hard swift strokes to the bank. (*He "swims" to behind the sofa*) Heaving yourself beside your round-bottom'd white-gold milk-breasted oh h h h gh. (*He gulps; rubs a hand across his mouth*) Smoothing your giant brown hand over her piquant belly to that venus-fluff-sweet-cherry . . . oh-h-h-h-gh! (*He swings round, his back to the sofa; then slides slowly from view to the floor*)

A long pause. George sniffs; continues fastening his braces on to a pair of trousers. But after seconds have ticked by without Albert's emerging, George peers over the sofa back; then he rises, and edges around the sofa's L end. He peers down at Albert

George Mm. You've come up in my estimation. Who makes the pills? Trade secret? (*He is deeply impressed*) Albert, you *are* a giant. Sexual zest at your age! Couldn't pray for greater glory, you couldn't. God's glory. (*He stands to attention*) I salute you, Albert. Couldn't pray for greater glory. You'd best have it off: it's sapping your strength. (*He moves in front*

of the sofa; sits at its L end, then continues buttoning braces on the trousers)
No. (*A frown for himself*) You are winning, Albert.

Albert appears and, kneeling, leans upon the sofa-back, chin upon his folded arms

Albert *Only*, George—I am *only* winning *if* one accepts that achievement or progress—call it mentality, is God's biggest accident; and financial security, God's worst disease. (*He scratches his nose on his cuff*) Then yes, one could claim that my potent, middle-aged carnality was the only natural glory; whilst all this, ah, luxury was merely a disease. (*He nods his head at the room around*) A nasty disease.

George Thank you. And here's me, fastening your braces on your trousers for you.

Albert I am not considering a god born of man: I speak of the real God. And to Him, luxury is a disease and sex is ah—yes, an everyday joke. To God, little man with his piffling parts has no more significance than maggot or carrot or tetanus bacilli. . . . Oh yes, I'm human; but it is no comfort for me to be a sexy maggot when *you* are a successful one.

George Get your hands off the brocade. You'll make it greasy.

Albert rises. He fastens his shirt cuffs

Albert It's so silly. Alicia prays, you see. She prays if one of us is sick: prays for God to kill the germ. It is one God's thing praying for another God's thing to be murdered. Germs have as much right to kill man as man the germs.

George Did you tell Cheryl you liked her puddin'; her puddin', did you?

Albert (*sitting on the sofa*) Ah, I said it was quite nice pudding, yes. I'm not mad on hot soufflé, though.

George Well, curse my germ-riddled home.

Albert Anyway, I told the surgeon, on my oral finals at medical school. I said bacteria had as much right to kill people as people bacteria. And he failed me.

George He felt you preferred disease to patients.

Albert Alicia prays for a baby, George. A baby of our own. Yet it'll be close to medical history if she has one. So, to be on the safe side—and I've heard her whispering, she prays "Please God let Michael be Albert's son".

George Oh dear oh dear.

Albert She knows how I've anguished and anguished for Michael to be mine. And *I* have prayed, George. Oh yes. I have prayed for some god to erase that night when we all . . . when we all slept together. (*He slams one fist into his other*) The night we all of us slept in that same Dreadful Bed.

George Aw, Albert, you poor old maggot. (*Compassionately, he rests his elbow against the sofa-back, his hand to his brow*) Poor, sad maggot, scrabbling in your darkened chemist's shop; the racing years twisting your heart out. Oh dear oh dear. . . . Aren't you over it? After nineteen years? Alicia's over it, isn't she, isn't she?

Albert Alicia is an especially sweeet, naïve person, George.

George (*hotly*) Well you're a poor sod; and she should've given you a baby.

Albert Her problem is in the ovaries, George. Alicia is all woman, George. Dear me yes! Oh, Alicia is quite hot stuff.

George I knew Alicia, Albert: knew her when she was Alice; so don't tell me how hot Alicia's stuff is! *I know.*

Albert I refute that. It is very unkind. You are belittling our women to protect yourself.

George ⎫   I am not.
Albert ⎬ (*overlapping*) Yes you are.
George ⎭   I am bloody not.

Albert You are. You are!—to explain how Michael is the only baby from when we were all in bed together, *and I was on the scene.* But ever since I left the scene, you've had nothing but wall-to-wall-carpet and naked soldiers.

Slamming the dress trousers into Albert's lap, George rises. He takes the brandy goblets to the table UR

George Put your pants on! Get your mind off—*things.*

Albert (*taking George's trousers from the sofa-back*) I'll put the braces on your trousers.

George You will hell.

A childish struggle develops, each hanging on to George's trousers

Albert ⎫   It's nothing. (*He rises*)
George ⎪   Get off! Get off!
Albert ⎪   I want to, I want to
George ⎬ (*overlapping*) You fiendish sod.
Albert ⎪   Let me, let me!
George ⎭   NO.

George wins

No bugger on earth does anything for me. *I* do for George. *Me.* And what I need, I *make* happen.

Albert Oh, we've been puppets on the string of that woman of ours.

George Of *ours*? Now who's belittling?

Albert Michael was *my* baby, George.

George He was mine.

Albert He's going to be a doctor; and that is in *my* blood.

George And who checked the blood of us both, eh?

Albert My heart died when it came down tails.

George I gave you blood, I'm saying.

Albert I know, I know.

George Sample after sample. "Can I have another sample, George? *Yes.* Yes. Another sample can I have, George? *Yes.*" Fatheaded chemist who can't analyse a spoonful o' blood.

Albert We both have agglutinogen B. I told you. Eight in each hundred have agglutinogen B; but it has to be us two. *And* we are both rhesus negative. (*Picking up his own trousers, he strides to* C, *and shouting at the gods*) Go on, laugh at me! Whistle at me!

George We kept you out of prison, us three. *Prison.* A chemist who poisons people. You nearly murdered us all.

In a flash of temper, Albert hurls his dress trousers into a corner

Albert Blast you to hell! And blast your riches and your wife! (*He strides to George*) You destroyed me. That cup is mine. (*He hurries to the mantelpiece. He seizes the trophy*)
George (*throwing his trousers on to the sofa*) Get off me cup!

He runs across, grasps Albert's hands; and—in their dishabille—they perform a macabre ballet, quarrelling in a circle, childishly struggling for possession of the trophy

Albert I'd've been ballroom champion.
George Could've been a giant and a doctor. But you weren't.
Albert You cheated me, cheated me.
George Give me my cup, you mad sod!

Round and round they struggle, panting, grunting, and hissing insults. At last, they pause—winded; yet neither will relinquish the cup

Albert You cut the buttons, you cut the buttons on my dancing trousers.
George (*gulping*) You're—a damn liar.
Albert Half-time. . . . I went to the showers, didn't I . . .? Half-time, I went for a quick shower; hung my trousers over a curly Victorian peg. God, how I've dreamt this moment over and again and again.
George And God curse you for a liar.
Albert Why did *you* come into the shower?—you, who hadn't washed his feet in a year.
George You what! I was a clean youth, *clean.* Gimme my cup, my cup . . .

Another struggling circle

Albert (*close to hysteria*) You cut my buttons; you severed my threads—the threads of my life. Say it, say it, SAY IT!
George I'll say sweet Fanny!

With a final wrench, George wins the cup. And he cuddles it, as mother with child. He mutters and glowers, and polishes it against his chest. Pause. Albert retrieves his trousers from the corner; George replaces the cup, then moves across to the sofa for his own trousers

Albert I—I apologize, George. Brainstorm. Sorry. (*He dons his trousers*)
George The girls'll be down soon for our bednight dance.
Albert I watched Michael throughout the summer—meeting a pretty little girl at the bistro opposite.
George That'd be Deborah. I gave them the cash.
Albert (*yearningly*) Marvellous.
George Pom-pahdy-pahdy-pom-pom . . .
Albert And by standing on our shelf ladders, I could see them at a table. "My son" I'd whisper. But our giant apothecary bottles made him distorted, in pink and yellow and green.

George Jesus, I shall weep. Soap commercial, is it?—with your dreamin'n hating, and blaming *me*; and your giant god's balls shriekin' for freedom. (*He has fastened his braces wrongly*) Oh 'ell! If you're trapped in your vinegar bottles, smash the buggers. Smash 'em, and *make* life happen—like me. I make it happen. I wouldn't cringe in a screwed-up ointment shop. (*He cannot guide the button into his braces button hole; he flops into the sofa*) Grr. And you're not the only sod who dreams, either. I see *myself* with crystal maidens and fat-tittied virgins, shieldin' *my* eyes against the hot white tundra.

Albert Tundra's Russian.

George It's still flamin' hot.

Albert No no no, s'cold and white.

George Knowall.

Albert Minarets and vodka. (*He sits beside George*) Dostoevsky. And there is always a shot in the orchard. Yes!—there would be a shot in the orchard. Cherylovna, bleeding in the grass. Cherylovna, beautiful wife of Georginov—the rent collector. Ha ha ha. (*He rubs his hands*) This is how *I* dream, George.

George You do. Uhugh.

Albert Drifting snow and wolves. The old mother on the stove. And Cherylovna, white and fading. And the surgeon, hours by droshky in Petersburg. *Who will save her?* And save her child?

George Albertinovsky!

Albert God, George, the glory. The glory. Having you all kiss my feet as I operate. How will he do it? *No instruments.*

George Nothing but a shoe horn and a Jewish samovar. I know. I know. And I know something you don't know.

Albert What?

George You'd bloody kill her.

Albert (*nodding*) Yes. Yes.

George Belly-achin' dreamers. Cheryl's the same. Cheryl fantasizes. Good days, she's Carol Lombard. Bad days, she's all hot'n sticky from Tennessee.

Albert (*rising*) Well, the orchard is silent. Cherylovna married George. And Albertinovsky lived hauntedly ever after. (*His attention is drawn to the trophy; tensely*) I live over and again that tortured moment. Hear them hooting and jeering and clapping.

George Don't start don't start!

Albert And I'm back in that ballroom, doing my double-chassis with these trousers around my ankles.

George Think o' something else.

Albert (*savagely donning his tail-coat*) *We*'d've won that cup. We were the best couple, you know we were.

George (*rising to struggle into his trousers*) Were you hell.

Albert And always your face zooming-zooming-zooming through my sweat and tremors. And that knife in your hand. *Your penknife.* (*He swings to stare at the cup*)

George Touch my trophy 'n I'll have your pinkies with a bloody chopper.

Albert How could *both* back buttons go? Both back buttons. *Both!* (*He moves towards the trophy and stands on the rug*)

George Aw, bugger both your back buttons. You lost the cup; lost your baby; and now I can't get my shoe down my trouser-leg, wouldn't it rip your giblets, goddam.

Albert Why are you so torn apart if you are innocent?

George Because! Oh, I shall dress in peace. (*He grabs his tail-coat, and hobbles into the hallway one leg in, one leg out of his trousers. He turns*) And get your hooves off the goatskin *RUG*!

George exits UR

Albert follows to C, *frowning*

Cheryl enters down the stairs, happily singing. She is resplendent in a magnificent ball gown—typical of the competition dancing of her day. Its flounces are crisp, its colours radiant—as though it were recently purchased. She goes to the fireplace

Cheryl Darling-darling Albert!

Alicia follows down the stairs, and as always—in her faded, crumpled, old and ill-stored gown—seems sad by comparison.

Isn't your Alicia a kitten? Pirouette, Alicia-dear! Show Hubby what he owns.

Alicia, pleased with herself, pirouettes, ending on a sickly curtsy

Isn't she delicious!

But Albert is shocked. He looks from one to the other. And he touches the material of Alicia's gown

Albert Oh no! I shall tell George. This is not fair. It is not damn fair. We shall not suffer this outrage.

Angrily he exits UR

Alicia bursts into tears

Alicia He hates the memory; hates my fr-frock; and hates our Dreadful Bed Night.

Cheryl He's in a silly tizzy, darling. (*Absently, she plucks fluff from Alicia's gown*) Frustration, sweetie. Rumbling frustration. Albert *is* frustrated, Alicia. He *is*, darling. That chatter through dinner—about life in his big vinegar bottles. Well!

Alicia (*fresh tears*) Oh-ogh-ogh.

Cheryl Oh hell, you are a silly bee. Yowling like a ninny. Darling, *I* shall settle Albert. Here!

She guides Alicia towards the easel

You look at my divine Welsh corporal. (*She throws back the easel cover*) Cheryl will sort everything out.

Cheryl exits UR

Left to herself, Alicia's weeping escalates. She sobs loudly, bitterly. But at the height of her sobs, she turns to gaze upon the painting. Her tears vanish in mid-yowl—as a child, when offered a candy bar. Alicia studies the painting uneasily. And, as though trespassing, she tries to avert her eyes from pelvic places—but cannot

Alicia (*to herself*) Ooooogh.

Cheryl enters UR

Cheryl The boys are squabbling. Man stuff. We don't care. Isn't he adorable? And my dear   he ran everywhere like that. Threw off his tiddly uniform. "How d'ya want me, girls!" Delicious. Course he was, well, respectable; *but* there is always one silly bitch storms out. Mrs Thingy from Twilight Lane stormed out. (*She sinks among her frills into the sofa*) Very next day six new housewives joined. Ha! So what do you think, darling?

Alicia (*glazed*) Pardon?

Cheryl Of my bloody painting, darling.

Alicia Oh. It seems—(*she steadies her voice*)—it seems sort of off-centre.

Cheryl Well it would be, dear. He's dancing.

Alicia sits beside Cheryl

Course he isn't finished. Don't suppose he ever will be, 'less I can find another man in the village. Do you know anyone?

Alicia Like him?

Cheryl Yes, like my Welsh corporal.

Alicia (*firmly*) No-o-o-ogh. (*She giggles*) No. Wouldn't there be someone at George's bottle factory?

Cheryl No, I've been all through the bottle factory.... Leather aprons'n jowls; all gristle'n feet. They have the delicacy of a stallion's buttock. (*Shuddering*) Urrrgh. Oh no, I want Bacchus. The girls want Bacchus. We've started on Bacchus. God, I shall have twelve shrieking cats on Wednesday; and no man. (*Rising, she waltzes to* C) Oh, darling, my Welsh corporal *was* Bacchus. He was *any* god—because, God, he was beautiful. So lithe and potent and *raw*. Ooogh, I wanted to ... we all wanted to ... every second I wanted to—Oggggh. *How dare* they steal those soldiers from me—(*quickly*)—us.

Alicia Perhaps you could do some jugs and flowers and stuff.

Cheryl Just because we're housewives is no reason to fart with jugs'n flowers. We have flesh, hot'n sticky, real young flesh. And we do very nicely.

Alicia Perhaps they've left a little sentry behind.

Cheryl We don't want a little anything, sweetie. We want Bacchus with his neck and chest and stomach and flanks and thighs. Ogggh, my corporal was sheer Michaelangelo; and I shall never forgive the bronze bugger for leaving me—us. (*She flops back on to the sofa*)

Alicia S'a problem. I can't imagine anyone in our village who'd, um—well, stand naked and—ooogh!

Pause

Perhaps George?

Cheryl George who?

Alicia (*quickly*) Your George.

Cheryl (*flabbergasted*) George! What an awful thing to say. George—naked. Oh no. *I mean, I* want to paint. *I* want to paint. And I'm the Chairwoman, sweetie. I'm Chairwoman. When the girls have gone, I . . . well, I clear up.

Alicia Don't you have a daily woman?

Cheryl I *pay* the boy, Alicia. We have to pay poor soldiers, for Lord's sake, dear. So I make a little drinkie and cakes; and ogggh, it's *delicious.* (*She hugs herself*) Delicious. (*A deep sigh*) Oh how I yearn to leap naked into honey; and have Apollo toss me a chain of diamonds, a *chain*, then cling in ecstacy as he draws me up . . . (*she rises slowly to her feet*) . . . hand over godly hand, up—up—up—*up* to Olympus: to be ravaged by Greeks, baring—themselves. (*She warms to her fantasy*) Standing proud at the helm. Hair in the wind. Golden reins to prancing stallions. And me, in the Queen's white chariot; naked breasts in wafting chiffon. Rampant Apollo, laughing as I slash off the heads of my suitors. (*Again, she hugs herself*) Delicious. Delicious.

Alicia has shrunk further and further into a corner of the sofa. Now, Cheryl turns and sees her

Back from the gods to Alice. (*She sits beside her*) Darling, you mar the furnishings. Why are you cringing like a whipped budgie?

Alicia (*rising; piqued*) You were sizzling enough at school; but now! You must be threadbare. All threadbare inside.

Cheryl I am warm and loving inside, *Alice.* Why are you so cold and wet, *Alice*? You are so weepy, you have put dear Albert's fire out.

Alicia (*attacking*) You forget: I knew you when you were Cora Crutcher, Cheryl. So if you don't drop this sudden *Alice*-stuff—next time we pass at the hypermarket, *Cora*, whilst you are pretending the butler is sick, *Cora*——I shall shout "Hello Cora Crutcher! Did they send back your knickers from the scout hut?"

Cheryl rises quickly. But she swallows her temper. Smiling icily, she moves UL

Cheryl As you will, *Alic-ia.* War's over for tonight, *Alic-ia.*

Alicia There's no war. I couldn't compete. Ever since we were young, you've used me to make yourself look better. No, I *am* the crumpled type. . . . I really envied you when you were ploughing through the scout troop. I couldn't even conquer Chuffy Gosport. He said my behind was like an ironing board. Still, I did get Albert. And *you* wanted him, didn't you?

Cheryl bursts into laughter

Cheryl (*moving to the fireplace*) I was so anxious, I tossed a coin to see who'd be father.

Alicia I know how you tossed; and I know what you were after.

Cheryl What *was* I after?

Alicia George's factory and the silver cup. And you stole them both—because it's *my* silver cup.

Cheryl "defends" the trophy with her hands

(*Laughing*) But you *wanted* Albert; and you lost him.

Cheryl I would have made Albert great. With me behind him, he'd have a thousand drugstores now.

Alicia And you could've spent your life painting them. It's all your talent's worth. You couldn't dot the eye of a tomcat's bottom.

Cheryl Hoh, this is pure Alice Trowton.

Alicia You've given that poor soldier a cockie like a salami.

Cheryl You *are* a cunning, weepy-violet, *Alicia*. (*Crossing towards, the easel*) But you are mixing with your betters, when you tackle me. (*She giggles*) For heaven's sake, darling—I have already "enjoyed" your Albert. As far as we remember.

Alicia As far as we remember. But since we were all drunk in the Dreadful Bed, we shall never know.

Cheryl (*replacing the cover on her painting*) Yes! Wouldn't one have thought a mother should know. But I don't. (*Comically*) Every year we speculate, don't we?—on who slept with *whom*.

Alicia (*strongly*) Whoever, whatever, Albert is mine. And even if you once did, you won't again.

Cheryl My sweet—(*she walks towards Alicia*)—if I needed your Albert, I could take him, send him to that glory he craves; then spit him out.

Alicia You could not.

Cheryl (*facing her*) I could have him posing like my soldiers. All bare. Our pompous Albert, all bare; and then——!

Alicia ⎫	You could not.
Cheryl ⎬ (*overlapping*)	Could.
Alicia ⎭	Couldn't.

Cheryl Darling, you *asked* me to paint him.

Alicia In flowing robes against a molten sun.

Cheryl Well I'd have him naked.

Alicia ⎫	You couldn't
Cheryl ⎬ (*overlapping*)	I could.
Alicia ⎬	You couldn't, you couldn't.
Cheryl ⎭	I could, I could.

Alicia I BET YOU.

Angrily, they are face to face

Cheryl Oh? (*She circles around Alicia; pondering*) What would Mrs Chemist bet with? Corn plasters?

Pause. Alicia considers nervously

Alicia With gold. I should bet with Albert. Because, if you won . . . (*sadly*)

... well, you'd've had your prize, wouldn't you? (*Spiritedly*) What does the Madonna of the Bottle Factory bet with?

Cheryl Oh, who lit your fire today? (*Crossing to the fireplace*) How would you snatch at gloves and shoes to that old dress'n handbag I gave you?

Alicia Gloves and shoes for Albert? No-ogh. No, I'd want matching handbag, gloves'n shoes, to your three Majorca outfits in the cream and beige and green.

Cheryl Bloody 'ell! (*Sweetly*) Is that all?

Alicia No. Your camel'n leather coat, as well. Oh!—and that gorgeous suede continental jacket.

Cheryl Good God!

Alicia With matching handbag, gloves and shoes, of course.

Cheryl My camel'n leather is new. It's nearly all new, sweetie.

Alicia You see! You can't afford Albert. (*She turns away airily*)

Cheryl (*clapping her hands*) DONE. (*She meanders across Alicia; then speaks over her shoulder*) So, I make Albert pose naked. And any nonsense on the side—is mine, as well?

Alicia Um, (*swallowing*) yes. Just for t-tonight.

Cheryl S'a bet. (*She swings round*)

Alicia And all the matching hats, too.

Cheryl Any other oddments?

Alicia That reindeer hide suitcase for carrying home m-my—my winnings.

Cheryl (*merrily*) You saucy bitch.

She spits on her palm; so does Alicia; and they shake hands

I'm beginning to like you. (*Compassionately*) But, sweetie, don't you know Albert is drowning?—in the dark of your *fading* shop, among those huge vinegar bottles.

Alicia crosses to sit on the sofa; she begins to weep

Alicia He's j-just a teensy middle-aged.

Cheryl And hungry and itching—like me.

Alicia He's not.

Cheryl He *is*, darling. And why weep? There're no men to watch you.

Alicia I'm f-frightened your camel'n leather won't fit me.

Albert enters UR, *followed by George, who stops beside Cheryl*

Albert (*storming authoritatively*) We have been insulted. Change your frock, Alicia. We are leaving.

Alicia Oh HUSH, Albert!

Albert (*shocked*) Alicia!

Alicia Hush—pet. (*She falls back on her customary weeping*) We don't w-want them to s-see we care, Albert-pet.

George Isn't that beautiful? Her little face.

Cheryl Oh, but look at Albert's cheeky face. (*She kisses his cheek*) There. All better, sweetie. (*She fusses over to Alicia, then sits beside her on the sofa*)

George Kissing *his* cheeky face! Nineteen years ago, he damn near killed us. (*To Albert*) You'd've hanged if we'd died.

Albert I didn't know that little bottle was on the poisons list.

George Wish we had died—so you *could've* hanged.

Albert I was tipsy. We were all tipsy.

Cheryl All I remember is darling Albert saying he could make whisky.

Alicia He can. He can.

George I woke up sightless. "I can't see, Mother," I cried. Three days, I was, with a white stick.

Albert Give over, George.

George My one flash is *you* giggling like Frankenstein over frothin' bottles.

Albert Don't exaggerate.

George My glass was smoking.

Albert (*shrugging*) I made a little mistake.

Cheryl It was a bomb while it lasted. Who'd ever have dreamt of sleeping with two men *and* Alicia!

George This brave, proud darlin' ... (*sitting on the sofa-arm, he hugs Cheryl*) ... was four weeks in hospital.

Cheryl And pregnant when she came out. (*Fondly, she pats his knee*) Put on *our* slow foxtrot, George.

George moves aside the glass table. Then he puts a cassette into the player (or record on the turntable). Alicia rises to UL, *and takes a dancing stance with Albert*

But, darling Alicia what *are* you doing? (*She rises*)

Alicia Same as every year. Going to dance with Albert.

Cheryl Ah but, sweetie, *this* year it must be as on the Night of Our Dreadful Bed.

George is pulling aside the sofa

George Hellfire, Cheryl!

Cheryl George-darling, it was you and Alicia who won the cup. *I* was with Albert when he lost his trousers.

Albert, Alicia and George begin talking at her

(*Moving* DR) Oy! Oy!

They stop talking. George starts the music

That is the way it was; that is the way I want it. (*She sings*) Alber-er-ert ...!

She beckons to him. Albert, seemingly mesmerized, walks dance-style out of Alicia's arms and into Cheryl's. George takes up his stance with weeping Alicia; the Lights fade to three spots and the couples are dancing in and out of these spots as——

the CURTAIN *falls*

ACT II

The same. Ten minutes later

On the glass table is a tray with coffee pot, cups and such

When the CURTAIN *rises Albert stands* LC *sipping coffee; and George is fussing with an ornamental brush and pan, sweeping up crumbs (especially from the carpet around Albert's feet). Albert moves away to the fireplace. To George's annoyance, he puts his cup and saucer on the mantelpiece in order to finger the trophy. Albert turns, and—catching George's fierce glare—steps over the goatskin rug, and moves behind the sofa. Absently, he plucks at the sofa-back, whilst surveying the room. George drops his pan and brush* UL. *And with his handkerchief, he polishes the trophy and wipes beneath the cup and saucer. Then he returns Albert's cup and saucer to the glass table. Albert progresses* UR—*to fiddle with a statuette (on a plinth between the table and pillar); George now straightens the sofa-back. Albert returns to stand behind the sofa* C; *and George follows to his* L

Albert I always feel out of bounds in your mansion, George. (*Nodding at the easel*) Like our Shrouded Warrior.
George No-one's stopping you looking, are they?
Albert Aha. (*Moving to the easel, he throws off the cover. He raises his eyebrows; amazed, he backs away to beside George again*)
George Jealous?
Albert Ah, medically speaking, I'm astonished.
George And?
Albert Hmm. As an erstwhile doctor, I should say you have a problem, George.
George I'm very worried, Albert.
Albert Mmmm.

Pause

There's a lot between the lines, George.
George There's a lot between——oh 'ell! What should I do, Albert? What should I do?

Albert in-draws his breath. It is a long in-drawn negative with raised eyebrows.
Pause

Albert Is he dancing?
George S'not finished.
Albert He'll thrash himself to death.

Pause

George S'very alarming, Albert.
Albert I'm glad it's not my problem, I must say.
George Comforting.

Albert makes a frame of his hands, to view the work professionally

Albert It is ah, too explicit for Cubism. . . . Closer to Dadaism. . . . With a touch of the Gothic.
George Oh well that helps.
Albert M'yes. Sepias are building tolerably; and her sub-tones are not unacceptable. No ah, when Cheryl has finished her Bacchus; and ah, reduced the outlines . . .!
George The outlines get bigger.
Albert Hardly seems possible.
George We've twenty like him in our rumpus room. Each bigger than the last.
Albert Do you mean ah, the same soldier?
George No, the corporal's new. But we've a William and a Terence and a Kenneth and a Fred, and on and on. All getting bigger.

Pause

Albert Mmm. Cheryl needs a hobby, George.
George This *is* her hobby, you nut.
Albert No no no no.
George Needlework, you mean? *Knitting* for the troops?

George breaks away; Albert follows

Albert The soldiers are gone, George. No soldiers; no temptation.
George Aw, you upset me earlier, with your Scandinavian titties. (*He crosses to the glass table*) How can you be lusting and lusty all the day long? (*He turns*) You're *not*, are you?
Albert I have ah, a relatively constant prickle, George. (*He rubs his stomach*) And—not entirely pleasant, a thoracic anticipation, as it were, in the peritoneal layer.
George (*hotly*) Your coffee'll be cold! (*He hands Albert his cup from the glass table*)
Albert Ah.
George Oh 'ell, I lied. (*Moving all round the sofa*) I lied. I *lied*. I LIED.
Albert I'm sorry?
George That cheeky bottom at Radlett's: when I told you, and you ran up the walls in ecstacy—with your sexy maggot business.
Albert Aha?
George I said I was *viable*. But I lied, Albert. Oh, I noticed the minx and her bottom, but my ho-ho-ho's and skittles'n beer'n tickle'n grunt—*lies*. I was keeping my end up, as a hoary old bugger like me is supposed to.
Albert M'yes. Perfectly normal, George. One must accept a certain diminishing of the ah, acetyl-choline, the ah, spermatica plexus.
George Bloody 'ell! *Your* plexus hasn't diminished. It's blasted immortal. (*He strides upstage and back, anguished*)

Albert And we ah, experience no pungency whatever, old lad—in a cheeky
bottom?

George Nobody *should* at our age. We're not whistlin' young and steaming
any more.

Albert I still consider myself a connoisseur of bottoms, George.

Albert moves along the glass table; and George follows him

George I'm not saying bottoms aren't beautiful. A bottom's a beautiful
thing.

Albert God wot ...!

> Fring-ed pool
> And fern-ed grot;
> Yet there are fools who say
> God is not.

George (*glowering*) Have a drop o' black in there! (*He tops up Albert's cup
from the coffee pot on the glass table*)

Albert sits on the sofa; George slumps beside him

I need reassurance, Albert. I can't remember being young. I see a
bottom—and yes, it's pear-shaped'n chubby; but it's only where a body
breaks into legs.... For God's sake, Albert, am I an exception among
middle-aged fellas?

Albert No. *I* am. (*He laughs; but he changes quickly to a fierce intensity, his
jealousy shining through*) I should diagnose *power*, George: the strutting in
your glory; your striding and fuss and bang, your contempt of accolytes;
and your thick pile and flock paper, George. Your power has sucked you
dry.

George (*plaintively*) Oh 'ell.

Albert (*leaning back*) So, possibly Fate is balancing the scales for me.... I
am mostly medicines now: hypermarket's stolen my business. It's hours
between one "Hello, madam" to the next. My sole excitement is in the
flash of a storm, when thunder rattles my pills, and lightning flecks the
phallic bottles. Yes! I could write soliloquies upon bottoms. Ah ...

> A beautiful thing is a bottom,
> A bouncing and pear-shap-ed thing.
> Its curve and its sweep and its jobble,
> With the split and the chubb and the swing.
> Ah ... the judder and wibble and wobble;
> Oh-h-h-gh, a bottom's a beautiful thing.

George *Put your cup down, it's Royal Worcester!* (*He grabs Albert's cup and
saucer; puts them on the tray. Then, he rises, and strides to the easel*) I
couldn't come within years or muscle or hopes o' this damn whistling
corporal. (*Wistfully*) Be wonderful if I could. But I can't. (*He replaces the
cover; then moves above the sofa*) Albert, I'm losing Cheryl. I can't match
her pace, old darlin', her pace. You talk of *your* unfulfilment! I have the
unfulfilment of an aborted sneeze.

Albert I daresay one man's sneeze is another man's cough mixture.

*Alicia hurries down the stairs. She looks charming in Cheryl's camel-and-
leather, with matching hat and gloves and shoes*

Alicia Have you boys left any coffee?
George All yours, darlin'.

Alicia lifts the coffee tray from the glass table. Radiantly, she smiles at Albert. Then she exits upstairs

Albert Alicia? (*He rises, following her upstage*) Alicia! (*To George*) She wasn't wearing that coat when she came, was she?
George Don't you know your own wife's frocks?
Albert Wasn't it one of Cheryl's?
George God knows! (*He glares*) S'only Cheryl's "still-warm rags o' Sheba". Doesn't concern you.
Albert I have an excited skin. (*He shivers*) A constant sense of rumours tick-ticking. A touchy pelt, as though all my nerve ends were gossiping.
George Not surprised. With your lust, you should be covered in warts. . . . Even as a lad, I wondered how long sex lasted. Not the act—the condition. (*He moves to Albert; confidentially*) Do you ever remember Busty Cora?
Albert Do I ever! Oh-h-gh, fifteen and sizzling There was a bottom for you! And titties fit for milking time. Did you know she was raped over a tombstone, and the clergy hushed it up? Oh-h-gh. Wherever did Busty Cora go?
George She dyed her hair and called herself Cheryl.
Albert Oh Lord. Sorry, George.

George crosses and flops into the sofa. Albert follows, and sits beside him

George We are brothers at the feast, darlin'.
Albert I was tactless. I'm very *very* sorry.
George And she's been hottin' up again, recently: doing her hot southern belle bit.
Albert Very, *very* sorry.
George You didn't ever come with Chuffy Gosport'n me, did you—smoking in the organ loft?
Albert I—I wasn't in your choir, George.
George Oh. But it wasn't just the choir. Cheryl or Busty Cora, worked her way through every male from postman to the vicar. Came to church in tennis togs. Tight, white panties. And when she stooped for a fallen hymnal, you saw curling heaven from our choir stalls.
Albert Really. (*He coughs*) Well well.
George She plagued the vicar wretched. And Chuffy Gosport'n me, we heard the vicar prayin' for strength. "I am unblest," he cried. "I am visited by randy goblins, all-horn-ed, winking from my pulpit." True. "Oh my God," he cried. *"I want her, I want her, I want her."* Do you see what my wife has done to us all?
Albert Feel you shouldn't tell tales out of church, George. He *was* your vicar.
George Hellfire—he was Man! And Cheryl was Woman. And I'm failing and fading.
Albert What ah, what did he do? The vicar?

George He grew very thin and old-looking. . . . I remember one of his eyes broke out.

Albert tut tuts awhile

Chuffy Gosport'n me were terrified. If holy men were like this—what would *we* be like when *we* were middle-aged? And now I'm terrified because I'm NOT like the vicar. Oh 'ell! (*He rises, to pace behind the sofa*) No, I respect that old holy ram. A good lad, he was. A true man o' God's nature. (*He leans over the sofa back; in a hoarse whisper*) She seduced my builder. He made her a secret room in our studio roof.

Albert In your paddock? A secret room?

George A secret love nest. In the rafters. She thinks I don't know. Albert-darlin', I'm frightened to know. But I've peeped inside. (*He hurries upstage to ensure no-one is listening. He hurries back*) Up a little ladder. There's a blasted ottoman and hangin' tapestries. And joss sticks. Oh, Albert, (*desperately*) I cheered inside, hearing those soldiers had gone. But now I'm trembling for who she'll turn to next.

Albert (*worried*) Oh dear, dear dear.

George (*grabbing Albert's arm*) I won her, and I mustn't lose her. I couldn't. *I can't.* Help me, Albert, help me.

Albert Yes um, um. We must *pretend*, old lad. And hint, yes, *hint* at deep fires inside you.

George What if she takes the hint? I'm tired. Tired.

Albert Well ah, m'yes ah, when *I'm* tired——

George (*frantically*) Oh, don't advise me on what *you* do, you lecher! It's like Apollo recommending his photographer. (*He strides up and down*) Easy to laugh with pearly teeth. Try laughing with cankered teeth. Show me a man who laughs with cankered teeth; I'll show you a saint. It's a brave man who laughs with cankered teeth. On the other hand . . . (*he pauses, bewildered by his own logic*) . . . what sort of man laughs all over the place with cankered teeth? Should have 'em fixed. Oh, I'm so confused. (*Now, he eyes Albert suspiciously. He leans across the sofa-arm; pugnaciously*) All through our hot soufflé, she was devouring *you*.

Albert (*rising worriedly*) I know, I know, *I know*.

During the following, Albert is backing away from George; all around the sofa

George Why did you say Cherylovna in the tundra?
Albert I didn't.

George		You did.
Albert	(*overlapping*)	No. No.
George		Yes. YES.
Albert		All right, I did.

George WHY?
Albert Because I want I want *I want her*.
George YES.
Albert Fantasy, George. Nothing sexual.
George The hell it isn't: you want *her* and she's after *you*.
Albert No no no no.

Albert turns and moves away; but George hurries to the front of him DL

George (*stopping him*) Look, I'd do anything to win. Anything. I hate myself, but it's the way I am. So naturally, I judge you by the same standards.

Albert I would not machinate behind the back of a friend.

George Great, because a whistling corporal's one thing; but you're another. And you, with your days in your bottles in the dark, and *me* with my rowing machine—I reckon I could lick you, Albert. (*He holds a fist beneath Albert's nose*) I reckon I could lick you, darlin'!

Cheryl enters downstairs, carrying a fresh oil canvas and paintbrush

Albert Heaven forbid, George, heaven——

They turn and see Cheryl

George Ah, there we are, darlin'!

Cheryl My two sweeties, chin-wagging in dark-brown-leather.

Albert Chatting, yes, chatting.

Cheryl is looking particularly alluring. She has changed into an exotic, expensive leopard-skin outfit of trousers and tunic and baubles. She slinks to the easel, replacing her soldier with the new canvas

Cheryl Babies, caught with your fingers in the marmalade pot. Cheeky boys! (*She slinks to* C, *smiling; then stopping, and directing her leopard-skin bottom at the men, especially Albert, she pushes her soldier under the* L *end of the sofa*)

Albert is tempted. George raises his fist in warning

Mmm, I feel so animal in these delicious trousers: hot and wicked like a deep southern belle from an old fried-chicken home.

George (*hoarsely*) Oh 'ell!

Cheryl poses against the sofa-back, the paintbrush held cigar-fashion between her fingers

Cheryl Down in the everglades all among the passions an' the poor white trash; n'the hounds'n hooch; ceegars'n women'n loins'n baccy'n spit. . . . (*She slinks towards Albert*) And the harlots'n gators'n swamps, you-all. And the molasses and rum'n sweat'n armpits on the ol' Bayou! (*She snuggles her back close against Albert, speaking over her shoulder at him*) Thar ain't nothin' past y'ere tonight, boy. All them bridges is down . . . dow-own. . . . (*Slowly, she slides her back downwards and then upwards against Albert's side*)

Albert moans. George is close behind Albert and, glaring, he pulls Albert away upstage. Albert retreats behind the sofa; but Cheryl slinks after him

And just who d'ya think you are, 'cos you-all set yo' seed in the belly of a New Orleans jezebel? Think the world'll ever call you great? (*To George*) Fetch ma whusky an' ma gun!—and I'll teach him glory, honey. 'Cos he ain't nothin' but a drea-eamin' man. (*Reaching behind her, she strokes Albert's face*)

George moves ominously, so Cheryl turns her attentions on him, whilst Albert retreats further R

Ma ol' daddy built these y'ere pillars; an' he crooned to me in his ol' rockin' chair. I can ree-member ma baby lips a'hangin' on ma mammy's great teats, like the green bitch-calf I was. (*She strokes George's cheek, then backs away from him towards the pillar*)

George moves UL

But I grow'd sweet an' strong. An' ma breasts grow'd fat with ambition for glory, glory-glory. I hear them trumpets a-callin' for ma ol' sweet-dreamin' . . . (*singing, and beckoning*) Alber-er-er-ert!

Albert raises his arm. He moves towards her. But George breaks the spell

George You rude hussy!

Cheryl—laughing, running, exits up the stairs

(*Following angrily to the bottom step*) I'll wipe the spots off that trumpetin' leopard, you rude hussy. Do you hear? Do you hear? (*He moves to a pillar and rests against it, shaking his head*) No discipline. No respect for me, Albert. I've lost my position. Hellfire! She'd've been lynched in Alabama. Her husband would've set her arse on fire. (*He comes into the room*) Well I warned you. And . . . I'm very ashamed, old darlin': having you subjected to that display. See how I suffer, do you? I'm so very, very ashamed.

Albert Yes, you have a problem there, George.

George Oh let the world have her! Soldiers. Sailors. Firemen. *You* can have her if you want her.

Albert No, no, really.

George Go on, take her, take her! Get your knife and fork!

Tentatively, Albert pats George's shoulder

She's hot-blooded, poor darlin'. Hot blood, she has. That's where Alicia's such a fine little wife. No ragin' beauty an' a mite faded; but nice.

Albert I should not describe Alicia as faded, George.

George No, divine, divine. Sweet little face. My big mouth, big mouth . . . Oh, *people are so damn rude today*. (*He shakes his head*)

Albert sits on the sofa-arm

My mammy and pappy, to this very moment—course, they're senile now, but I never heard my mammy'n pappy say a single rude word. Same for me as a lad. And I'm not sterile or impotent. (*Loudly*) Wax candle, I am, in a blast furnace.

Albert M'yes, m'yes.

George Have a care for that sofa-arm, would you!

Albert slips into the sofa. George sits on the pouffe

I was courtin' a little darlin' before Cheryl. Mary Jean. Seems yesterday.

British Grenadiers on the bandstand. Summertime'n bees. I was too young for the War, so I'm not all *that* old-fashioned. But when I was courtin' sweet Mary Jean, testicles and titties were *rude*. They were *rude*, Albert.

Albert Except as specific medical statements; or on statues, you mean.

George Um, yes. . . . And testicles were *very* rude. Oh, you could tempt ardent stars from a virgin's eyes with a cheeky tickle. And I mean a "tickle" of words. . . . I shall never forget those first shining eyes of Mary Jean. She thought I was so *marvellously rude*. And it was so charmingly *naughty*.

Albert Still quite welcome, George.

George It's animal, yes; but it's all so damn *bare*! (*He rises*) Oh Albert, so damn far from the days of Mary Jean, when we fiddled-for and giggled-for, and found those round, sweet secret places. (*Briskly*) Did you catch a sight of Michael's, um, girlfriend at that bistro?

Albert Only in wobbly pink and green.

George Michael's shacking up with that minx. Art student. Her eyeballs are bubblin' with hashish. I wish he hadn't found her. You wouldn't be proud of him, Albert.

Albert I had heard.

George And even when he gets to university—will there be doctors o' dignity in flowin' gowns? Will there hell. Ivy-clad traditions, innocent maidens?—will there *hell*!

Albert *Exactly!* (*He rises; vehemently*) Which is why I am sickened by the mediocrity of this greedy, rude and snarling world. And why I damn you to blazes for making me jealous.

George (*taken aback*) God Almighty!

Albert Now do you see why I yearn for glory?

George (*angrily*) Hellfire! (*He relents*) Albert-darlin', you *had* a chance for glory. You had airs of a young Einstein as a lad.

Albert I am not Jewish, George. I've told you I am not Jewish.

George Aw, fine, darlin', fine. (*He slumps into the sofa*)

Albert But I am not. Wish I were. I should have been brilliant. The Jews are the greatest, most talented race ever known. Politicians, sculptors, scientists, everything: there is no profession on earth which is not crowned by Jews. Any genius—Freud, Disraeli, Samuel Goldwyn, Al Jolson—and he is Jewish. But I am not. I'm not.

George Haven't been too many Jewish popes.

Albert My mother had moody, smutty eyes. A Welsh darkness. I am a throw-back, no doubt. But do you know, a waiter once refused me pork sausages at medical school? "Your dad wouldn't approve," he said. Everyone listening, George. "Kindly give me those sausages," I demanded; but he refused. I tried to hit him, George. But the other students held me back.

George Oh dear oh dear.

Albert I wish with a pain of heart I'd been born a Jew, because I should have had a positive aura; and known where I was headed. But I wasn't. And I haven't. And I don't.

George You're fine as you are, Albert.

Alicia hurries down the stairs, carrying a bundle of hats. She takes them off
UR, *then returns; smiles radiantly; and goes back upstairs*

(*Rising*) What's she up to, your missus?
Albert Alicia!

Alicia reappears. This time, she is dragging a heavy suitcase down the stairs

George Mind the pile, darlin'! Hellfire. (*He hurries to her*) Where d'you
want it? Front door?
Alicia Would you, George? Thank you awfully.

George carries the suitcase off UR

Alicia comes down to Albert

Albert Are we leaving? Whose is the bag?
Alicia Cheryl's—for the time being. (*She neatens Albert's white bow tie*)
Albert—no, don't look at me!—you have been gold's-worth and dia-
mond's-worth, and silver and wine and honey's-worth to me. You've
yearned in our chemist-shop; and grown older, and worrieder; but you are
a leader of men, Albert.
Albert Oh no no no.
Alicia Sssh! You are, Albert-pet, you are. And you'll never know how I've
prayed to be witty and suave—instead of a sort-of crumpled lady clown.
No, sssh! But I have always been just inside the shadows in case you
needed me. So you have just to shout, Albert. You have just to shout.
Because I love you.

She kisses the puzzled Albert

George enters UR

George (*from the hallway*) Is that *our* reindeer hide portmanteau?
Alicia At the moment, yes. Oh, George, Cheryl said you'd show me your
new studio in the paddock.
George Did she, the darlin'. Oh good. Good.

Alicia joins him in the hallway

Swedish maple, y'know. Redwood and glass. Northern light; marvellous.
(*He assumes the obligatory lechery*) Just off for a quick cuddle, Albert, ho-
ho. Oh—and if you smoke, use the glass ashtrays. The onyx'll mark. And
don't poke the fire—it's electric.

George steers Alicia out UR

*Albert moves to the hallway, and stares after them awhile (still puzzling over
Alicia's words)*

And he is unaware as Cheryl comes down the stairs, wafting a silken scarf

She oozes to one of the pillars; Albert is startled to find her posing there

Albert Ah, Cheryl.

Cheryl Is this where they stable the prancing white stallion?
Albert (*laughing obligingly*) Oh ha ha. Yes.

She surveys him alluringly

Cheryl I see memories.
Albert Yes, memories. Yes.
Cheryl No flashing recollections? No realization it was really *you*—or George—on our Night of the Dreadful Bed?
Albert Every year you taunt me, Cheryl; every year I *beg* you: have you remembered?

She smiles enigmatically, then moves into the room. Albert follows her urgently

Do you not love George?
Cheryl Darling George is a pet. I never kept pets, though: only slaves. (*Into his eyes*) I love hungrily and too well, I think. S'hard for me to be consumed by one love. But I've been lovely'n lively. Affectionate. And I've steered George to the top. We have laughed, and we have quarrelled with fun.
Albert Perhaps that *is* love.

Cheryl fusses at her easel, briefly, unnecessarily

Cheryl Do you love, Alicia?
Albert Oh yes.
Cheryl Yes. (*She smiles*) She wasn't supposed to warn you.
Albert I'm sorry?
Cheryl Alicia wants me to paint you tonight.
Albert Oh good heavens, ha ha.

Alarmed, he backs away. She follows him to LC

No no. One day, perhaps, ha ha.
Cheryl Tonight *is* one day. Hold your head higher!
Albert No no, really. Now now, ha ha.
Cheryl Sweetie, your face is tight'n grumpy. You have a cheeky face, my darling Albert. You should exercise it. Loosen! Open your eyes, darling. Wide. Wider. Stretch your mouth.

Albert obeys her instructions good-humouredly

Drag your eyeballs from their sockets. Make them cold. Your eyeballs'll feel cold. (*With her hand flat against his chest*) They feel cold, don't they?
Albert M'yes, so they would. By stretching your inner caranthus from the caruncle, one automatically . . .
Cheryl Does this feel warm? (*She blows against his neck. And then she wafts her wrist beneath his nose*) And can you smell my fascinating new *parfum*?
Albert (*coughing*) Mmmm'yes. Yes ah, Cheryl.
Cheryl Mmmm, that head! (*She adjusts the angle of his head. Then with her finger tips, she soothes his temple*) That tiny pulsating vein. Hidden powers. Arrogance. You have a lustful head, darling Albert. Sssh, hold

still! (*She backs slightly. She rests against the sofa-arm, hands prayer-wise to her lips*) Would you care to be a new Bacchus for my housewives?

Albert (*laughing*) Scraping the barrel because your soldiers have been posted? Ha ha, naughty!

Cheryl S'not naughty. My group is achieving recognition. We have three schoolgirls from the Council.

Albert Schoolgirls?

Cheryl Petal cheeks and bursty-free buzzies. S'quite horrid, but they give us status.

Albert I cannot believe the Council would send schoolgirls.

Cheryl You've heard naughty tales. S'not true. We are frightfully proper and you'd make a delicious Bacchus.

Albert Me! Bacchus! (*He laughs*) Dyonisius, born from the thigh of Zeus. And why?

Cheryl Mmmm. (*Rising, she walks around him in circles, arms behind her back, fingers sometimes wiggling*) Because you are sweet and sexy. And for the hell. Hold up your head! For excitement'n novelty. To escape from your nasty old shop of bottles. Pretend my ladies are Grecian trollops.

Albert Ho ho!

Cheryl Orgiastic rites, rivers of wine'n hot figs. Actually, we have coffee and buns.

Albert I prefer Alicia's Arabs. I ah, might be an Arab tonight, shielding my eyes against a molten sun.

Cheryl Chin up, chin up, sweetie!

Albert backs away slightly

Albert No, Zeus's thigh is too young for me. And the only hot figs *I* know are a laxative.

Cheryl Then we shall paint you *after* the orgiastic years, with carrots for figs. But the wine could still flow, darling. How would you fancy Old Bacchus?

Albert (*frowning*) How old?

Cheryl Young-old. Mind-old. Interestingly old; (*moving closer and closer*) interestingly *your* age, Albert.

Albert A dangerous age.

Cheryl Mmmm.

Albert I must look at your new studio with George and Alicia.

Cheryl Off you go, then!

Her lips are close to his. He is tempted, but stops himself

Albert Yes.

He backs away from her, then turns towards the hallway. But she catches his hand, and leads him into a dance

Cheryl (*dancing*) Have you ever wished it had come down heads? I have.

Albert I've wished Michael were mine.

Cheryl Never wished *I* was yours, and Alicia George's?

Albert Ah now, Alicia was always my girl. She was only George's dancing partner. George didn't have a woman.

Cheryl snuggles closer, holding him tightly

This is immoral, Cheryl. It is ah, quite immoral.

Cheryl Don't we fit snugly? All the ins and outs.

Albert I was never a dancer. Ah—oh—ah, no, George was the dancing boy. But it was you he was after. He wanted you.

Cheryl You wanted me, too.

Albert I was not keen, frankly, on Alicia messing around ballrooms.

Cheryl You want me, too, I said.

Albert Well, when a young man dances with a pretty girl. . . . No! No no!

Albert pushes her away. She twirls away to arm's length

(*Guiltily*) Freud said dancing and kissing were ah, representations or substitutions for the ah, act of ah . . .

Cheryl Mmmm, they are.

And she twirls into his arms again, her back to him and his arm tightly cuddled to her bosom

And we nearly won, Albert.

Albert YES WE DID.

For an excited moment, they whirl round and round in the dance

George was puce, ha ha! The semi-finals; and *we* were winning. (*He stops suddenly, his face crumpled by those old frustrations*) But my braces buttons snapped. I shall never forget.

Cheryl Mmmm. (*Huskily*) But what sexy legs you had, Albert.

She runs her hand down Albert's thigh. He pushes her aside, and stands away from her

Albert Now, now! This is wrong. You are a magnificent woman, Cheryl. Lord's sake you are. Dear hot-and-lovely Cheryl. But my frustration is for those growing years I lost. Gone. Dead! No little boy to understand, to fight for or worry over. *Little Michael was mine.* But now he is *grown*; and I am pained by urges to join his new learning and dancing and nudging. But I never shall. You and George created his growing days with me as a laughable uncle. (*Sadly*) Bacchus would never have been such a mortal flop.

Cheryl Then we shall alter Bacchus. Make him mortal like you. S'only a silly paper god. So we'll mould him into Albert against a sizzling sky. Raging, failing in blood-red. (*She demonstrates a pose—legs astride, arms stretching high*) Legs astride. Arms stretched to Zeus. Your tragic, sexy face in agonies of hopeless yearning for yesterday's son-that-never-was; yesterday's girls'n drinking'n singing. Zeus help me! *Zeus help me!* (*She tilts her head in frustrated agony*) God, this is *delicious*. What a delicious pose for a MAN!

Albert I see how you snare your soldiers. And ah, what would I be wearing for this exhibition?
Cheryl Naked, sweetie. You'd be naked.
Albert M'yes. (*Doubtfully, he in-draws his breath*)
Cheryl Just try the pose.

Before Albert realizes what is happening. Cheryl has helped him out of his tail-jacket. She places it on the sofa-back

Albert Cheryl! No no. It's the man undresses the woman.
Cheryl Mmmm, delicious. (*Invitingly she returns to* LC, *her back to him, her arms held high*)
Albert On principal, I meant. (*He retrieves his jacket; puts it on again*) I cannot wait here whilst you undress me. And I cannot stand naked for giggling ladies.

Albert goes round the R *end of the sofa; but Cheryl follows him*

Even my backside would be blushing.
Cheryl My ladies are artistes. Wives and mothers.
Albert And three virgin schoolgirls.
Cheryl Ha! We haven't had a virgin since that new motel at Whoresville. They're teenage *women*. Darling, you should thank me. Oh please, Albert-sweetie, please please please!

Pleading, she backs him to LC

Albert No. *No.* I am ah, I am not umblemished.
Cheryl (*understandingly*) Oh darling. Scars are *in*. Proves you are human'n not a sterile god. We don't worry over scars. If you saw some of my ladies, they'd be stitched haggises.

Cheryl senses he is weakening; she kneels at his feet

Sweetie, we shall put mothers to the front, girls to the side; and your tootie will be hidden by your best foot forward. (*She pulls his foot forward*) Or all at the back, and me at the front. You don't mind *me*?
Albert I cannot understand Alicia.
Cheryl (*rising*) She knows, Albert.
Albert Alicia *knows*?
Cheryl (*nodding*) Knows the plan for painting you. (*Intimately linking his arm*) And oh, what a delicious excuse for afterwards. For sharing secrets. *Please, Albert, please.* There is a secret heaven up some steps in my studio.
Albert Oh heavens.
Cheryl There is a little window peeping across fields. And nobody knows. *I'm stifled, Albert.* (*Whispering*) But it's glorious in my little place. *Come with me.* You wanted glory!
Albert (*weakening*) Napoleon commissioned a naked statue of himself.
Cheryl Mmmm, course he did.
Albert And he was of ancient Tuscan nobility.
Cheryl *You* are a noble man, Albert. A quick, smooth, *clean* man. And I shall make you *magnificent*. (*She eases behind him, pressing her hands to*

his chest. She speaks urgently, feverishly and convincingly) Darling, I'll give you the world. Yes, we'll show the world, Albert. Show them you're better than silly soldiers and their whole horrid army. Think glorious; think Bacchus'n hot figs'n rivers of wine; and glory, glory, GLORY! Try the pose, sweetie. Try it! Try it, Albert-sweetie! Try it! *Try it! TRY IT!*

Albert YES! *(On a sudden impulse, he shoots high his hands—his legs astride—fingers reaching for that molten sun)*

Cheryl, moaning, slides to her knees, hands slipping from Albert's chest, down his body to his thighs. Until . . .

Oh good God, what am I doing!

But Albert cannot break free from Cheryl, who clings to him. He staggers, then collapses full length across the sofa. Cheryl scrabbles on top of him. They struggle—round, behind and over the sofa. All the while, Cheryl is screaming, snatching, tugging, scratching and tearing at Albert's clothing. Eventually, Albert reaches safety behind the sofa. Pause, whilst Albert pants for air. His tail-jacket has lost a sleeve, is torn up the back, and a pocket of his trousers has been ripped to the knee. Albert's shirt, too, is shredded

Cheryl *(kneeling on the sofa; pleading)* Alber-er-ert!

Albert No. I cannot pose naked for all those housewives. . . . I've made up their eye drops. *(Dismayed, he examines his tattered state)* Made up their stomach powders, ladies' pills; served them quick drafts on hot days; heard their troubles; advised on their children, veins, husbands, piles and feet. *(He points at the "dais")* Good Lord, they'd say—*it's the chemist!* *(He lowers his pointing finger) And he's Jewish.*

A long pause

(Retrieving a missing shoe) And how long the engagement on this male model lark?

Cheryl Until always, darling, always.

Albert No ogh. I should be a novelty act for the interval, until "Hello, sweeties!" And in would come a glistening new fireman or farmer's boy.

Cheryl Never. Never!

Albert Women gushing. Schoolgirls rushing.

Cheryl I love you, Albert. I always loved you.

Albert And the red-faced backside of a village chemist, creeping for the exit. *(He leans to her, hands upon the sofa-back)* We are old, you and I.

Cheryl But I want you, sweetie. I want you want you *want you!*

Cheryl grasps his hand. Warmly, she kisses it. But Albert struggles free

Albert *(angrily)* Give over! You're sick. *Sick.*

Cheryl gives a strangled cry. She tears her nails into the sofa-arm

(Regretting his outburst) When I said "old" ah—no, no, you look beautiful, Cheryl. I meant in mind. Yes, you look so—so fresh and alluring and ah . . .

Cheryl *(screaming)* And *old.* *(She throws cushions at him)*

Albert No! Young. You look *damn* young. You do. You look, oh, you look *damn damn* young.

Cheryl You'd've been rotten, anyhow. Pins'n needles; or you'd've been cold'n blue'n pimply, or gone all red'n silly. You'd've been horrid. Urrrgh.

Albert Yes. Yes, I would. (*He rubs his brow with puzzled expression*) But now I have grown up—which is what old George was meaning. I yearn for impossible glories; for girl-children of milk breast and peach bottom—when my own backside is so very *un*-young as the God's-little-apples-that-once-it-was. What a shabby degraded fellow I am! (*He reaches a decision*) Yes. You are a lovely woman, Cheryl. And I am glad for your hobby and your soldiers. Yet, if you'll forgive me, there is no heart in them. No heart. No love. Your soldier under there—you have poured sheer God into that mother-and-father of all pelvises; but your corporal is empty inside. Yes. YES. (*He claps his hands*) When I get home, I shall take a hammer to those damn apothecary flasks.

Cheryl Psychology from a circumcised chemist.

George and Alicia enter UR

George Hellfire! Has she had you? Has she had you!

Alicia Oh no! No-o-o-o-gh.

George You hussy!

Cheryl exits UR, *George chasing after her*

Alicia slumps into the sofa, weeping bitterly; and Albert, groaning, rests against the mantelpiece, head upon his arms

    Cheryl returns. Beside her, a bewildered George is carrying the open suitcase

From behind the sofa, Cheryl grabs an armful of clothing from the suitcase; and drapes it over Alicia's head. Then she takes the suitcase from George, and dumps it beside Alicia. George helps take the clothing from Alicia's head. But now, Alicia is laughing. She is drowning in luxury, and through several delirious seconds, she sets hat after hat upon her head in delighted succession. George starts re-packing the suitcase

Albert Oh Lord! (*He wrings his hands helplessly*) It's spasmatic hysteria. Yes, spasmatic hysteria. Don't worry, Alicia-pet. (*Turning on George*) What have you done to us, you two? What have you done!

George I've done nothing, that's what I've done. *What did I do what did I do what did I do?*

Albert You cut my braces buttons. Say it!

George I—did—not—cut—your—(*deep-breath*)—BUTTONS.

Albert scrutinizes George's face; then he turns to Cheryl who is sitting on the pouffe. She shrugs unhelpfully

Alicia It was me cut your buttons, Albert.

Albert is stunned. He tries to speak, but can form no words

George You little darlin'. (*He roars with laughter*)

Albert My own wife. Destroyed, by my own wife.

Alicia Not then, I wasn't, Albert-pet. And you were falling for Cheryl, Albert. She'd always fancied you, pet. And if you two had won the cup—! But I knew Cheryl'd never go for a loser. So—I cut your buttons, pet.

Albert But, Alicia, my whole life's pattern was altered. (*Anguished, he goes upstage*) My whole life's pattern.

George Was it hell. That cup was mine by right. I worked for it, practised for it. Ask Alicia. Didn't we slave for it, darlin'?

Alicia Day after day.

George Week after, month after. Then up pops Albert and shuffles into the semi-finals. And why?—*because of her*! Because of Cheryl. The judges were lusting for her. Lusting—like *you*.

Albert (*to Alicia*) He put you up to it, didn't he?

George Did I hell. Why should I?

Albert Because you'd do anything to win. You said so. Your whole family was rotten; and your father notorious.

George If they're not cursing me, they're cursing my dad. And what of *your* father?

Albert My father is dead.

George Yes; and long before he died. (*To the others*) People whistled when his father spoke. Not on purpose: they didn't know he was there. (*He moves to Cheryl*) And as for my personal Jezebel, with her knickerless loins'n steamin' armpits—I could vomit with shame. How damn dare you seduce that *enemy* on our own sofa!

George pulls Cheryl from the pouffe, and swings her upstage

Cheryl (*sincerely, with genuine fondness*) Darling George, I'd happily take you on our sofa. Or on the lawn. Or behind the Bendix. Or on, under or up the bloody stairs. Trouble is, George, you never want me anywhere. (*She goes and sits on the pouffe*)

George I feel so hellish decadent. And saying "decadent" made my teeth hurt. (*Mournfully, he leans against the mantelpiece*)

Alicia Didn't we agree to include the beige one with cherries?

Cheryl mouths two swear words at Alicia

Oogh, there's culture.

Albert Oh, I might as well die: inglorious and sad.

Alicia Aw no, don't, Albert.

Albert Might as well, Alicia. I'm sure to go unnoticed. Even if someone said a few decent things at my graveside, George'd whistle through the words.

George (*absently*) Pom-pahdy-pahdy-pom-pom—oh sorry.

Albert Yet some people: look at Charlie Chaplin. Multi-millionaire, and he checks out at a glorious ninety on Christmas Day. Gets more mentions than Santa Claus. . . . Bing Crosby, another genius, rich and mighty—and he goes in a golfer's dream, winning on the eighteenth. He's Up There now, singing and whistling down on me. (*He sighs*) I wish God had made me Jewish like Bing Crosby.

Alicia Wasn't Bing Crosby Baptist or something?

George Well, maybe Bing Crosby'll make Albert Jewish—like God.

Alicia (*out of the blue*) My father is Presbyterian. He'd die if he knew of our shame.

Cheryl Well! Aren't we martyred buggers? His father, her father, your father.... My coughing, spitting father raised us in an attic overlooking the docks. I had orange-chapped lips and wet drawers. The floor smelled of garlic'n feet; and from our heaven, we gazed upon the men's urinal in Grafton Alley. (*She picks up cushions, dislodged during the struggle, from beside the sofa*) Green cast iron. And my brother'n me used to watch the undertaker standing there. No hands. The undertaker would've made a fair Bacchus.... And if it wasn't him, it was the policeman's horse down there—back legs across a gurgling pond; with a stream of lemon froth to the coal yards. (*She laughs briefly*) My brother'n me were floating boats in it one day. (*She moves to George, placing a hand against his chest*) So, I wanted to be better; and rich and fascinating, with coiffures'n perfumes; with clean hands, and wall-to-wall winning men. And I've done not a thing wasn't damn God-natural.

George places both his hands on hers

Alicia A shame you forgot little people on your way up. Old folk and cripples and coloured folk and all the world's animals and unfortunates.

Cheryl I didn't forget so many. Look at you with my hats. I do hope they fit. Sorry if they don't, but it's not my fault. And I'm sorry for feeling young, when age is wearying others. Well *I'll* be senile one day, darlings; *but not yet, not yet.* So I'm sorry, but it's not my fault. (*She moves to Albert. Comically*) I'm sorry for soldiers, and foxes and nasty big rumps on horseback. And I'd like to care; but I can't. So I'm sorry, but it's not my fault. (*Moving* C, *and with deep sincerity*) I'm sorry for being white when other colours are suffering. But my father was a drunken bum, and my grandad a miner; and neither of 'em pillaged Africa or kept slaves. So it's not my fault, sweeties. It's simply horrid being dirty white, and I'm sorry-Jesus-sorry; but I can't help it, I didn't do it, and it's not my fault.

Pause. She looks from one to the other, defiantly

And I'm simply mortified I'm normal, sweeties. I don't need unisex'n flat chests'n leather'n pulpits-for-Sunday-women'n men-with-titties. So I'm sorry I'm normal. I'm sorry for cripples everywhere; sorry for being born whole; Jesus-Christ-sorry that I'm healthy and sexy and alive; *but it's not my fault.* (*And now, to a defiant climax*) I'm sorry for all that's wrong in this titty-tatty world; but I didn't do it.... *I couldn't help it ... AND IT'S NOT MY FAULT!*

Cheryl bursts into tears and runs upstairs

A long pause. George moves to C

George Don't reckon it's my thumpin' fault, either.

Pause

All I did this morning was get up.

Pause

And I've been blamed ever since.

Now, George fetches two coats from the hallway. He returns and hands them to Albert

You'll let yourselves out, will you?

Albert ⎫ *(together)* ⎰ Surely, no bother.
Alicia ⎭   ⎱ Yes we shall.

George Whatever you do is never enough. Everyone falters in the clinches. There was a Tosser Guthridge lived near Ma Calthropp . . . (*He thumbs in Ma Calthropp's direction. He winces*) Aw, I've sprained my thumb on that portmanteau—and it's my one for sayin' "God's in His Heaven". Tosser Guthridge. Nice lad. Bit clever.

Albert Tosser Guthridge was killed as a missionary.

George That's him. Spoke nineteen native dialects; and on his first day out, he irritated some religious fanatics, and they used his head for a football. First day out. Nineteen dialects. And his last words were "Bloody 'ell" in English. (*He shakes his head*) How's *that* for unfulfilment?

George mooches off upstairs, scratching his head

Alicia rises and Albert comes over to help her on with her coat

Alicia I've worse secrets than buttons, Albert.

Albert Oh Lord, have you?

Alicia (*nodding*) I happen to know George didn't touch Cheryl in our Dreadful Bed. I didn't want you to know Michael was your baby—in case I lost you.

Albert Oh Alicia, *I* knew George did nothing that night.

Alicia Not to anyone.

Albert I know. It was me, Alicia. All through the years, I've been afraid to tell you. But I didn't want Cheryl for the mother of my son. I wanted you, Alicia-my-sweetheart.

Alicia smiles radiantly

Alicia S'comforting, Albert-pet.

She helps Albert with his mackintosh; and then hugs him, her face against his shoulder

I firmly believe everyone's a success. We shall always be a success, Albert—if only for having other people thanking God they're not like us. (*She strokes her tummy. Confidentially*) And frankly, I have been praying quite strongly recently.

Albert Give over. You haven't!

Alicia (*nodding*) And do you know, Albert, I have a sneaking suspicion, a sneaking suspicion I might be—you know.

Albert Oh Alicia. Pseudocyesis, pet. Ghost pregnancy. I mean, almost-a-doctor and twenty years a chemist: I could not possibly be mistaken.

She raises her eyebrows; and Albert pauses thoughtfully

Let's go home, Alicia.

The slow foxtrot begins to play. They walk towards the hallway; then Alicia remembers her reindeer hide suitcase on the sofa. One hat has been left unpacked. Alicia goes for the suitcase; but Albert stops her. Instead Albert picks up the suitcase and the Lights fade to a pin spot on the trophy

They link arms; and they walk out through the hallway, with Alicia swinging her hat

CURTAIN

FURNITURE AND PROPERTY LIST

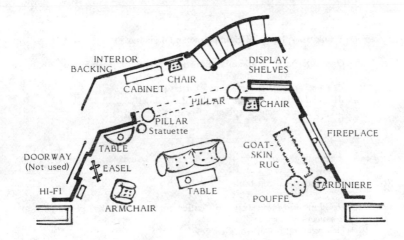

ACT I

Scene 1

On stage: Sofa. *On it:* cushions
Glass sofa table. *On it:* onyx ashtray
Armchair
Easel. *On it:* shrouded painting
Small cabinet. *On it:* hi-fi unit. *In cupboard:* records, cassettes
Console table. *On it:* framed baby photograph, tray containing bottle of
  champagne and 4 glasses
Pedestal. *On it:* nude male statuette
Small French chair
Display shelves. *On them:* nude male figurines
Fireplace. *In hearth:* electric fire. *On mantelpiece:* silver trophy
Goatskin rug on floor
Pouffe
Jardinière. *In it:* potted plant
Carpet
Pictures, flowers etc.

IN HALLWAY
Display cabinet
Small French chair
Stair carpeting

Off stage: Trunk containing 2 tail-suits numbered 18 and 19, 2 white dress shirts, 2
               white ties, 2 white waistcoats, 2 pairs of men's dress shoes, framed
               photograph (**George** and **Albert**)

Personal: **Albert:** pen-torch
               George: handkerchief

SCENE 2

Strike: Trunk, tray, bottle of champagne and 4 glasses

Set: *Over sofa-back:* 2 tail-suits numbered 18 and 19, 2 white ties, 2 pairs of
               braces, 2 white waistcoats
               At L *end of sofa:* **Albert**'s pair of dress shoes
               At R *end of sofa:* **George**'s pair of dress shoes
               On glass sofa table: 2 goblets of brandy

ACT II

Strike: 2 brandy goblets

Re-set: Sofa and glass sofa table C

Set: *On glass sofa table:* tray with coffee pot, milk, sugar, 3 coffee cups and
               saucers
               Dustpan and brush (for **George**)
               Coffee cup, saucer and spoon (for **Albert**)

Off stage: Painting canvas and brush (**Cheryl**)
               Bundle of **Cheryl**'s hats (**Alicia**)
               Reindeer hide suitcase containing assorted clothing (**Alicia**)
               Albert's mackintosh, **Alicia**'s coat (**George**)

Personal: **Cheryl**'s silken scarf

EFFECTS PLOT

Please read the notice on page iv concerning the use of copyright music and recordings

ACT I

Cue 1 › **George** starts the music   (Page 27)
Start recording of slow foxtrot

ACT II

Cue 2   **Albert:** "Let's go home, Alicia."   (Page 46)
Slow foxtrot begins to play

LIGHTING PLOT

Practical fittings required: chandelier and wall brackets in hallway; wall brackets each side of the fireplace and above console table, red glow from electric fire in room

A sitting-room/hall. The same scene throughout

ACT I, SCENE 1. Autumn night

To open: Darkness

Cue 1   When ready   (Page 1)
         Pin spot snaps on to trophy, then slow fade to full, warm lighting with all practicals on and coloured glows from upstairs and from each side of hallway

ACT I, SCENE 2. Autumn night

To open: Full warm lighting with all practicals (excluding chandelier) on and coloured glows from upstairs and each side of hallway

Cue 2   **George** takes up his stance with weeping **Alicia**   (Page 27)
         Lights fade to three pin spots RC, C *and* LC

ACT II. Autumn night

To open: Darkness

Cue 3   When ready   (Page 28)
         Quickly bring up full warm lighting with all practicals (excluding chandelier) on and coloured glows from upstairs and each side of hallway

Cue 4   As **Albert** picks up the suitcase   (Page 46)
         Fade to pin spot on trophy

MADE AND PRINTED IN GREAT BRITAIN BY
LATIMER TREND & COMPANY LTD PLYMOUTH
MADE IN ENGLAND